WHAT YOU DO IN THE WAR, GRANDMA?

D0314770

SOMERSET COUNTY FEDERATION OF WOMEN'S INSTITUTES

From John & Sheila

COUNTRYSIDE BOOKS
NEWBURY BERKSHIRE

First published 2005
© Somerset County Federation of Women's Institutes, 2005

All rights reserved. No reproduction
permitted without the prior permission
of the publisher:

COUNTRYSIDE BOOKS
3 Catherine Road
Newbury, Berkshire

To view our complete range of books,
please visit us at
www.countrysidebooks.co.uk

ISBN 1 85306 909 4

Designed by Peter Davies, Nautilus Design
Typeset by Jean Cussons Typesetting, Diss, Norfolk
Produced through MRM Associates Ltd., Reading
Printed by Woolnough Bookbinding Ltd., Irthlingborough

Contents

FOREWORD

A s I travel around Somerset visiting Women's Institutes, I am amazed at the stories that these women have to tell. They really did put the 'Great' into Great Britain. When their world was falling apart they buckled down, did jobs they had never thought of doing previously, travelled far from home in many cases, and held the Home Front together. I am honoured to be their County Chairman and I am thrilled that they have decided to tell us just how they coped in those dark, terrifying days of World War II. I hope you enjoy reading their stories as much as I have.

Veronica Andrews
County Chairman

ACKNOWLEDGEMENTS

W e are grateful to all the ladies who sent in their memories. Many felt their part in the war would not be of interest to others but, now they are all assembled, we feel we have a fascinating insight into what that special generation of women did to provide us all with the freedom to succeed in any chosen career today.

Our sincere thanks must go to Barbara Anscombe and Veronica Andrews, who, between them, have typed the whole manuscript.

Betty Knight, Co-ordinator.

4

CHAPTER 1

—⊷⚙⚙⚙⊶—

Women's Auxiliary Air Force

—⊷⚙⚙⚙⊶—

The Women's Auxiliary Air Force (WAAF) played a vital role in supporting the front-line activities of the RAF. The young women who joined up, or who from late 1941 were called up, found themselves in a new world of 'square bashing' (drilling) and 'jankers' (punishment) as they struggled to master the art of marching in step, saluting correctly, and receiving their pay packet without saying 'Thank you'. After training they could be working alongside male mechanics on fighter planes, plotting aircraft movement at Command headquarters, trying to control a huge barrage balloon – or even checking other servicewomen for nits! They all, though, had a special place in their hearts for the boys in blue, so many of whom never came back.

—⊷⚙⚙⚙⊶—

My greatcoat came past my calves
Gladys Brown, Templecombe

I was the first girl from the little village of Templecombe, Somerset, to join the forces. I enlisted in the Women's Auxiliary Air Force (WAAF) in September 1940, and reported to Bristol with three other girls I encountered on the journey. We were billeted that night in a private house and were allowed out to go to the cinema. After the film we found the street in an uproar. The

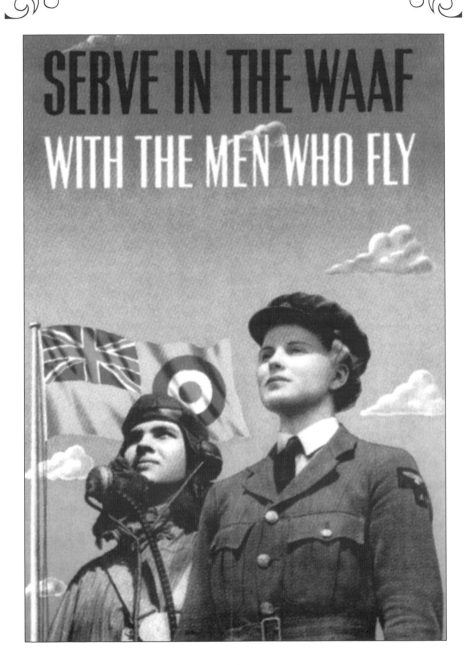

Gladys Brown.

air raid siren was wailing, the warden was trying to get people in various shelters, and he asked which was ours. Well, we didn't have one and in the panic we all forgot where to return to. Fortunately he could remember who took in girls from the forces for the night, so we arrived back much subdued.

Next day off to Harrogate, arriving very tired and hungry. We were obliged to queue for ages at the Grand Hotel for a room and bedding. No lift working and I shared Room 525 with other girls. I staggered up countless stairs with my case; two heavy army blankets; two coarse cotton sheets and something like a large swiss roll called a pillow. Square bashing the next day, and issue of uniforms. My greatcoat came past my calves, but 'in no circumstances must it be shortened' said the sergeant. Well, I wasn't wearing it like that; being only 5ft 1in can you imagine what I looked like? So, borrowing a pair of nail scissors, I hacked some off, when to my horror it left no room for a hem! I then turned it up a quarter of an inch and stitched it somehow, and no one ever knew. Incidentally, after being demobbed, if you sent your greatcoat back you were sent ten shillings, which I did.

Then it was the practice for pay parade. We were terrified. We had to march smartly up to the table, take our money with our left hand, saying the last three digits of our Air Force number, and salute, turn right and march back in line. Somehow we managed it. One of us said 'Thank you' and the sergeant was furious! My first Sunday away from home was spent dancing in the NAAFI with countless handsome partners. So different from civvy street where a dance was once a month and not nearly so exciting.

After Harrogate I was posted away for training as a flight mechanic, to service the aeroplane engines. The course was 18 weeks of hard grind, but oh, so worthwhile. The boys on the airfield where I was posted after the course were so helpful. We had a male corporal for each six girls. I worked on Spitfires,

Gladys Brown's discharge paper.

Hurricanes, Wellingtons and Lancasters. My pride to see the first aeroplane I had serviced soar in the air was great. I am now 84 years old but I can still remember that moment in time.

We wore battledresses and men's overalls, with leather jerkins to keep out the cold, and when in Scotland waiting for the pilot to come, the boys taught us sword dancing (minus the swords) to keep us warm. Once the ground was frozen and I had to go under the wings to pull the chocks (blocks of wood under the wheels) away as the plane prepared to taxi, but the wheels skidded and the plane swung round and I was knocked over – it could have been fatal but I survived, with bruises.

During training we had to stand on the fuselage and watch the pilot rev up the engine and note the gauges. We stood in line: 'A volunteer to be first?' asked the corporal. Muggins stepped forward – up on the plane beside the cockpit. Away roars the engine, but unfortunately the slip stream lifted my feet in the air and except for clinging on to the window with my finger tips I would have been blown back off on to the ground. I couldn't tell the pilot to throttle down as the engine made so much noise. He said afterwards he couldn't make out why I looked so deathly white. They all thought on the ground that I would be blown off any second. After that episode it was no longer included in training.

Some months later I had another terrifying experience. This time my own fault. Near where we were stationed there was a truck drivers' pull-in where gorgeous food was served – all hot and greasy, but so appetising after ours. So two of us sneaked down there on lunch breaks, nipping across the airfield. Unfortunately on this day the fog came down swift and ferocious. A plane rushed back to base and we had to fall on the ground sharpish. I'm sure it was only feet above us. My ears ached for days. We could so easily have been killed as, of course, the pilot couldn't see us. No one knew so we avoided being put on a charge to be followed by 'jankers'.

I had to go to hospital once as I developed appendicitis. It was a huge ward with 30 beds down each side: civilians one side, forces the other. The nurse would come each day asking if anyone had an egg they needed boiling for tea. How I envied those civilians who had relatives to bring them eggs. Then one day a priest came to my bed and gave me an egg – he had brought it for someone who had been discharged. Oh, the joy when nurse came round and I too could have a boiled egg for tea – one of the best meals of my life!

I belonged to the concert party. We travelled near and far entertaining our personnel. I tap danced and sang, etc; once we marched criss-cross on to the stage in uniform singing *Rose of England*. We felt so very patriotic. We made costumes from old parachute silk and dyed it, to quite good effect.

After the war I wrote to Filton aerodrome for employment, sending my references. The reply came by return – yes, come and see us. My parents persuaded me it really wasn't a job for peace-time for a girl, so I didn't follow it through, and returned to civvy street, working in a food office dealing with documents for service people who were being demobbed.

I had a wonderful time learning new skills
Kath Hutchings, Wivesliscombe

I left my employment at Fox's, Wiveliscombe on 4 September 1941 to join the WAAF and make my contribution to the war effort. Leaving Taunton railway station I made for Upper Hednesford to be picked up by RAF transport; one other girl was on the station as I alighted. We were both scared stiff, but soon became good friends.

Next day we went off to Blackpool to be kitted out and start our training – up and down Blackpool mile. We were lucky to have private billets in nearby Morecambe. The basic training continued for eight weeks, following which we were once again on our travels, posted to RAF Henlow to begin specialised training as Balloon Operators. It really was very interesting, but very hard work, especially when the wind moved and you had to

Barrage balloons proved a handful for most women.

move points. We were then posted to active duty in Southampton. On the night the city was 'blown to pieces' we had our first bit of good luck; that night we brought down a German plane, but, sadly we lost our balloon. I came back to Eastern Gordano, Bristol, still in the Balloon Command. Eventually, and with what we all thought was much needed commonsense, the RAF powers-that-be realised that balloon operation was too heavy a task for the majority of girls.

This led to a change of job as I was transferred to Bomber Command. Twenty-three weeks of training followed to become a fully trained Instrument Group 2 Worker. The training was just like going to college every day but I enjoyed it very much. It was a lot to take in as for all the planes you eventually worked on you had to sign a special form 700. This all took place at RAF Valley, Anglesey, where I stayed until I was demobbed in 1946. I had a wonderful time learning new skills, meeting new people and contributing to the whole country's resolve to defeat the enemy and retain our liberty. The saddest moments were always, however, when we lost as many planes as we did, along with the brave crews whom we got to know so well.

Home was a wooden hut

Joan Wright, Compton Dundon

I joined the WAAF at 18 years of age in 1941, when living at Milborne Port in Somerset. I was sent to Harrogate for initial training, and put into the Grand Hotel, which was so palatial, I thought how wonderful, but after two days of luxury we were sent to an RAF camp in or near Manchester, and 'home' then was a wooden hut, and it was January so very, very cold with no central heating!

After training as a teleprinter in the Signals Section, I was sent to RAF Titchfield near Southampton, where I spent some very happy times, and met some very lovely people. Work, of course, in a Signals Section was top secret, and shift work included night duties, enabling us to spend leisure time during the day. I

WAAF operators.

remember we would be invited to Netley Hospital which was American at the time, to spend social time with the patients, who were wounded American soldiers, playing cards or just chatting. It was there I met a soldier who gave me a copy of a book he had written called *Leave Her to Heaven*, and he told me a film was going to be made of it and if I had a chance, to see it, which I did after the war. I still have the book!

My most vivid memory is of D-Day. We were confined to camp with no reason given, but there was a strange quiet atmosphere around. Then hundreds of American troops arrived and were camped alongside the main road to Southampton, opposite our camp, complete with tanks and very large guns. On the morning of D-Day I awoke to the sound of aircraft overhead and on looking out of my billet window saw the sky was black with aeroplanes, each towing a glider. The news had not yet broken, but the Americans started moving out towards Southampton and Portsmouth, with messages on the side of their guns saying 'Watch out Hitler – here we come'. Later on, when the news came through of the invasion I was on duty at the Signals Station receiving messages on my teleprinter machine reporting the names and rank of the casualties killed or wounded on the beaches. I then had to transfer these messages direct to Whitehall on a special teleprinter machine which had been installed a few weeks earlier. A very sad task for a 21 year old girl.

I was given seven days' leave to get married
Dorothy Francis, Long Sutton

I joined the WAAF in October 1941 and went to Insworth, Gloucestershire, for my uniform. Two days later I was sent to Morecambe for 'square bashing'. After two weeks of this I was sent to Titchfield, a balloon centre near Portsmouth. Five months later I was posted to Madley in Herefordshire to work as a waitress in the Sergeants' Mess. While at Madley I was given seven days' leave to go home to Castleford, Yorkshire to get married. In 1944 I was posted to West Camp, RAF Cranwell, Lincolnshire as a waitress in the Officers' Mess. I was discharged in 1945.

Dorothy Francis.

I didn't fancy myself wearing khaki
Gloria Vercoe, North Petherton

I couldn't wait to reach my 18th birthday when I could 'join up' – the day after, I was first in the recruiting office. Birth certificate in my hand, I proudly said 'WAAF' when asked which service I wanted to join. This was my choice because I didn't fancy myself wearing khaki, the Wrens seemed only to offer boring desk jobs,

Gloria Vercoe

but the RAF was really glamorous, and I wanted to get as close as possible to those gorgeous Spitfire pilots. Hardly the fire of patriotism but a powerful incentive to a young woman hardly out of her convent school!

A preliminary medical was given and I was rather taken aback when it was my own family doctor I was confronted with. 'Does your mother know you are here?' he said – fingers crossed behind my back I said, 'Of course!' First hurdle passed and just a few days later my rail warrant arrived with instructions to report to RAF Gloucester. Luckily my best friend had joined up too and we travelled together. What a rude awakening for us convent girls – we entered a big hut with about 60 other females and were told to strip – and the WAAF corporal meant 'strip'. We shuffled round and eventually found ourselves before the doctor who gave us a brief 'FFI' (free from infection) examination and we thankfully dressed again.

The next three weeks I enjoyed very much – learning to march on the parade ground, which I loved: deciding which occupation I wanted to be trained for, no problem there, WAAFs were able to be mechanics so I reasoned that a mechanic I would be. Thus getting me the close encounters with pilots and planes I had joined up for. To achieve this ambition I needed to show an aptitude for putting square pegs in round holes and deciding whether a page of black lines was thicker than a page of white lines, and lots of similar tests which to my utter astonishment I passed and was accepted for training. After this I was given my uniform and all the necessary bits and pieces for keeping the badges, buttons and shoes gleaming. Woe betide anyone who failed to do this as I very soon found out.

Six months' mechanics course at a vast camp on Cannock Chase followed – I never thought I would make it. However, I did and was a step nearer to my ambition. A seven-day pass to go home before my posting and I was so proud walking along the road in my airforce blue uniform. Dancing was my passion, so off to the local palais, not wearing my usual 'glad-rags' and 3-inch heels but the 'uniform' and flat black shoes. Actually I was not too keen about being home, we lived just outside London and as the crow flies (in this case fighter planes) we were between two front-line fighter stations. There was plenty of action – not only from the RAF.

My first posting was to a fighter training station in Scotland, and there were the young pilots and the Spitfires, I couldn't believe my luck. There were just two WAAF flight mechanics and we were not at all popular with the male mechanics, but worse, the pilots weren't too happy about us either! They changed their minds after a few months when they found the WAAFs were just as competent as the men, and sometimes their fingers were more nimble. I found it a wonderful experience, even when the Scottish winter arrived and ice and snow had to be scraped off the planes before they could be serviced ready for the first flight – usually at 7.30 am! I was responsible for two Spitfires which had to be checked every morning. This involved revving up the engine to nearly full throttle and checking the instruments. There were only about five instruments in a Spitfire in those days, but to do this the tail had to be weighted or the plane would tip onto its nose or start to move off. To provide the necessary weight two colleagues would have to be cajoled into laying across the tail plane and bearing down whilst the engine was pushed to full throttle. Not the best of jobs on a freezing morning just after a breakfast of scrambled dried egg or kippers (this is Scotland remember) and strong tea. Still, we did this for each other and everything went smoothly – mostly.

The routine was to escort the pilot to his plane, hop up after him and check his parachute harness, slam the cockpit hood shut, jump down, pull away the wooden chocks from the wheels and call 'chocks away', giving a thumbs up sign. The pilot then switched on the engine and with a mighty roar, smoke and flame belching from the exhaust, he taxied to the runway for take-off. We flight mechanics then filled in the necessary flight log and waited around for his return. As our own plane landed we guided him to his parking bay with regulation hand signals, helped the pilot from the cockpit, tied down the plane and re-fuelled ready to start off with another pilot. Sometimes repairs and adjustments were needed to the engines so we did this too. I didn't like it very much when the cause was a bird, especially if a seagull had got caught in the air intake during flight – a messy job!

Life on this small fighter station was wonderful. There was such a great sense of comradeship and the social life was everything I had dreamed of in those far off civilian days – Saturday night dances in the surrounding town – Scottish reels and Scottish pubs – a weekend in Edinburgh – piping in the haggis amid cheering and stamping – cadging rides in a plane when it was being taken up on a test flight (strictly off the record this)!

Later I was at Hornchurch for a short time, which was exciting, being a front line fighter station, but I found it harrowing. Some of the pilots I had been dancing the night away with and made a date for the pictures didn't return from their mission. Only lads really, 19 or 20, younger than my grandson is now. It was just as well my stay at Hornchurch was short or I may have been quite badly affected by this.

WAAF riggers at work.

My next and last station was again in Scotland, only further north still, at Lossiemouth. This was a huge maintenance unit on the Moray Firth surrounded by beautiful scenery. Here I had to get used to working in a very different way – mostly it was servicing and repairing engines of big planes, Lancasters, Halifaxes, and Wellingtons which was carried out by a team of mechanics. I really missed my 'own' Spitfires.

The WAAFs were billeted in quite lovely hotels overlooking the golf links and sea, but I missed the close companionship of the 'huts' on my previous stations. During the war it was accepted that people hitched lifts with any vehicle going near their destination – usually a lorry. On one memorable occasion I hitched a lift, together with a dozen other service people, all the way from Aberdeen to Marble Arch in London sitting on boxes of kippers. From Marble Arch it was quite a short trip on the Tube to my home and I wondered why I was getting such funny looks. As I walked through my front door and embraced my mother she backed hastily away and said, 'You smell horrible, I know how you travelled home.' Well, there was a war on!

I was now hairdresser in charge of 904/5 Squadron
Joan Lee, Puriton

Six months before my 18th birthday I joined the WAAF at Colchester in Essex. There were twelve of us going to Innsworth in Gloucestershire, and although I was the youngest I was given the travel documents and was put in charge. This was my first journey on a train and to me Gloucestershire was a foreign country. I soon learnt the art of delegation and we all arrived safely, to be kitted out and to learn basic training. After two weeks we were posted to Morecambe for further training. Three weeks later I had my first posting to a unit. Complete with heavy kitbag on my shoulder I reported to the Balloon Squadron in Manor House, London. I was now hairdresser-in-charge of 904/5 Squadron, which included all balloon sites from Stoke Newington, Bethnal Green and East India Dock Road. My job was to check the girls for nits and lice. My 'salon' was in the boiler room of our billet, but when I went to the Sister it could be anywhere – once I worked in the coal-house.

One day on a site near Spitalfields I found a girl with nits. My job was to find the offending creatures, but the medics had to treat them. The next visit I found she had them again, but by now I had coaxed the medics to let me treat her. On the third visit she had them again so I asked the medics to check her boyfriend. He also had them so we cleared both people at the same time and our troubles were over.

One lunch time we were chatting in a room at the billet when a V1 landed in the next street and blew our windows in. Unfortunately, a WAAF was sitting on the radiator by the window and fragments of glass blew into her back. We got our tweezers and pulled them out while we waited for the medics. Another day two of us were in the basement when a V2 landed in the garden. It blew out the side of the house and killed the other WAAF. My bed was twisted beyond recognition but although I was pressed against the wall I was unhurt.

After a spell on leave I was sent to Biggin Hill where we slept in underground shelters, in double bunks. I had a lower bunk and one morning I woke to find the water had seeped in level with my bed. Everyone else had gone to work so I paddled out in my pyjamas and greatcoat and had to walk back to my billet past the men at work, who thought it was a huge joke.

We managed to make cottage pies and stews
Ellen Davey, Pawlett

I was born in the small village of Fishponds near Charmouth in Dorset. When I was 18 I went into domestic service in Lyme Regis looking after two elderly ladies. After a while I was joined by my cousin.

When I was 21 my cousin and I volunteered for the WAAF as I did not want to work in a factory or become a land girl. When the time came to leave I had to go to Dorchester for a medical but my cousin decided to go to Lyme Regis hospital. I passed the medical all right but my cousin did not, and I was eventually called up.

First I went to Innsworth Lane in Gloucester for training. Here we learnt how to march and salute etc. We enjoyed ourselves very much and had a good laugh because we didn't know whether we were saluting officers or WOs.

Next we went to Melksham to train as cooks. It was hard work but the company was good and we had a good time. After passing, some of us were sent to Pembrey and Burryport in South Wales as our main station. I worked in the airmen's mess. There were twelve of us there. We had the normal rations, of course, but managed to make meals such as cottage pies and stews. It was very hard work but we liked it.

While at Pembrey I had a cooking test with two sergeants asking questions. It didn't take long; anyhow, I managed to get through and became a LACW (leading aircraft woman).

Later I moved to Spittlegate near Grantham, where I made more friends, and from there I moved to Exeter. This was great as I could get home easily. However, it didn't last for long as I was posted to Tetbury, a very happy camp and there I made more friends who I still see occasionally.

We had to carve 100 legs of lamb by hand
Stella Phillips, Buckland St Mary

I joined the WAAF in 1940. With others I went to the recruitment office in Exeter. From there we travelled by train to Gloucester, where we were kitted out and did two weeks' training (square bashing), and from there those who wanted to go into catering went to Melksham for four weeks' training. From there I went to RAF Honington in Sheffield. This was a large 'drome for Bomber Command. Having been brought up in a military family the rigours of service life were not a shock to me. It was hard work and long shifts, especially on night duty. We had to carve by hand 100 legs of lamb and bone and slice many sides of bacon.

We would count the bombers as they returned, and often had to comfort the girls who had boyfriends who did not return. Occasionally we might have an easy night and we could while away some hours doing embroidery, which I still have. We also formed a concert party and would have a lot of fun.

It was at Honington that I had my first disastrous flight. We were not allowed onto flights from the 'drome, but two of us were dared to go by some of the pilots, who were taking part in what was known as 'circuits and bumps' (flying and landing at other aerodromes). These were in small Oxford planes. I have never been a good bus traveller, but this time I was ill. It taught me a valuable lesson – not to disobey orders.

Holme-on-Spalding-Moor in Yorkshire was my next posting. Our WAAF site was quite a way from the main 'drome and at one time we were isolated by snow, and food supplies were dropped by plane to us. We found that the people in Yorkshire were very hospitable and one family treated me as one of their own.

From Yorkshire I was next posted to Woolfox Lodge in Rutland. This 'drome was divided in the middle by the A1 road. It was easy to hitch hike from here. Next came RAF Tilstock in Shropshire, then RAF Hampstead Norris in Berkshire. This was, of course, the build up to D-Day. We were very busy in the messes as the numbers of airmen were boosted by glider crews (many American). We were not allowed out of the camp during this time, but had no idea what was going on. On the morning of D-Day I was on 4 am duty in the Officers' Mess, but there was an eerie silence and on looking out on the runways we found that it was completely empty of planes and gliders.

Hard biscuit mattresses and rough blankets
Lianne Beauchamp, Buckland St Mary

Having left Paris in July, where I had optimistically entered for a year's course in French, and having left most of my belongings behind, the declaration of war in September found me at a complete loss and the only course open to me was to join up. I was in London and stood in a long queue for the WRNS, but on looking across the road the queue for the WAAF seemed to be moving quicker, so I crossed over and my fate was sealed!

WAAFs getting to work on sprucing up an RAF lorry.

I was called up a couple of months later (meanwhile I filled in my time by making a warm dressing gown), and reported to an RAF training depot at West Drayton in Middlesex. I arrived in the dark and was conducted by torchlight through the hutted camp, which was surrounded by a high wire fence, to my quarters. The long wooden hut had a huge iron stove in the middle and eight iron bedsteads, each with a locker and a mat, ranged down each side, and 15 young women in various stages of undress, flimsy nighties and scanty panties, putting on face cream and putting hair in curlers!

Within a week we were all in warm pyjamas (was I thankful for the dressing gown), and after a quick dash to ablutions we tumbled into those beds (hard biscuit mattresses and rough blankets) completely exhausted. We were some of the earliest volunteers, and we were put through the same intensive training as the regular male recruits – PT, drill and marching. Poor

Sergeant Major – we were all in civvies, some with high heels, one carrying her handbag! On the march we either skirted round pools or jumped over them. After about two weeks of this the next step was an interview, where I was deemed suitable as a Plotter, and was posted to a fighter station in Lincolnshire. By this time we had been issued with uniform, complete with 'bloomers, blue' with elasticated legs.

The winter of 1939 was bitter; we slithered on icy roads to and from Ops to our quarters, which had been the married airmen's houses, four girls to a house. The bath was in the wash-house, with bath water heated in the copper which was stoked with coke (rationed) which we stole from each other's outhouses! We were issued with a mug, knife, fork and spoon which we carried with us to the Mess some distance away. Because we worked in shifts all through the day and night we were spared the parades and routine drill. It was tough, and it was only the camaraderie and the humour that made it bearable. At that stage most of the girls were from families in the forces or society girls (one had her horse stabled at a nearby farm!). It was all so new and unreal. We had to apply for a pass to leave the station, and had to be in by midnight. Of course we soon made friends with the fighter pilots, there were dances and ENSA shows on the station, and we met in the local pub or went into London.

The plotters worked in the ops (operations) room underground, round a huge table with a grid map of the country. We were connected up to the Observer Corps, who passed on sightings of aircraft, and we pushed blocks with flags giving information – x number of aircraft, height, direction – and the Operations Officer called up the fighters to intercept: 'Scramble' was the operative command.

After some months I was recommended for a commission and did an officers' training course for Code 1 Cypher. I went first to a rather tame supply unit, but learnt a lot, particularly about the RAF, the customs and deportment expected of an officer (much of it was still quite formal), and thanks to that dear old Signals Officer, we never put up a black.

Eventually I was posted as Code 1 Cypher Officer (but later transferred to Intelligence) to a new bomber station in

Plotters in the Operations Room.

Lincolnshire, with an operational squadron of Manchester aircraft. The abiding memory of everyone there is of mud. We all wore wellies and carried our shoes slung over our gas-mask bags. As the WAAF officers' quarters were not ready we, six or eight of us, were billeted out in the village. We ate at separate tables in a corner of the officers' mess and sat around the stove in the billiard room. I think many of the senior regular officers deplored this invasion, but the younger ones enjoyed our company and we came to know some of them.

I played the tin whistle!

Gwen Watts, Dowlish Wake

I joined the WAAF on 7 April 1940 and was sent to West Drayton, Middlesex for 'square bashing' (training). I was posted to Exning,

Newmarket to No 3 Bomber Command. I was billeted with a nice family; a lorry picked a group of us up each day en route to the office in a country house in Exning where I did shorthand, typing and general office work. My officer had to interview crews of Wellington and Lancaster aeroplanes to get their views on how to improve equipment etc. We were now billeted in Landwade Hall in the village and one thick snowy winter when walking to the office an enemy plane machine-gunned a group of us so we jumped into a ditch, luckily escaping OK. We had air raids in Newmarket and one day a friend who was having her hair permed and was attached to the perming machine, as it was then, had to get out to the shelter in a right mess.

I drove a car for the officer, which with no signposts was very awkward in the dark and I had to know all our five stations. Once one of the WAAFs had gone AWOL, so I was sent to London to fetch her back. We stayed one night in the Strand Palace Hotel, with heavy air raids, all night it seemed, but we got back to camp safely.

I was posted to Hereford (Credonhill), and took a physical training course at Loughborough University, and then had to get the WAAFs out of their offices on frosty mornings for PT. There were about 50 or so; they shivered. We also had a WAAF band, gave concerts and for marching, I played the tin whistle!

I was then promoted to Sergeant PTI. I had my own car and on trips into Hereford I piled in my friends etc – then petrol coupons stopped so we had to walk or hitch hike. I was sent on a Gas Course at Rollaston, Salisbury Plain, which was all about decontamination; I never saw the village in daylight, a lorry picked us up in the morning and took us back in the evening in the winter. We had to be prepared in view of the possibility of gas attacks.

After some time I was posted to Wittering RAF Camp, near Stamford. It was very high up and cold and windy. My job was administration and PTI. This camp was nearer to my home in Northampton so I was able to get home on my days off, by bus of course, or I hitch hiked.

CHAPTER 2

Women's Royal Naval Service

'Free a man for the Fleet' said the recruitment posters for the Women's Royal Naval Service (WRNS) and Wrens responded with a will. They worked on naval aircraft, manned the offices, and tracked incoming enemy planes by radar, working 24-hour shifts. Some went abroad and witnessed at first hand the terrible plight of prisoners of war in the Far East, while others ended up at the code-breaking station at Bletchley Park. Some even got to join the boat crew – and to wear that fetching sailor's uniform of square tops and 'square rig' bell-bottom trousers.

My Wren friends were the sisters I never had
Evelyn Lintott, Milborne Port

Because of my age I knew I would have to make some contribution to the war effort, and I didn't fancy factory work, so I was very happy to go into the WRNS. My work was in a pay office, and although not spectacular, it did, as the posters proclaimed, 'Free a man for the Fleet'. I found the life congenial. The work was acceptable, the discipline did not worry me at all and it was marvellous to have so many friends. Friends I made during those years have remained with me, and are only fading

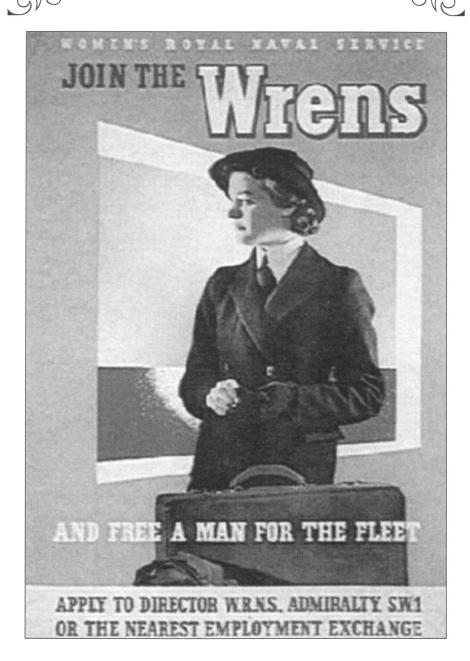

away now, because of age. My Wren friends were the sisters I never had, and I was very sad when demob came in 1946, but realised that service life and peacetime would be very different.

I wanted to join the boat crew

Jo Hirst, Tatworth

In 1943 I volunteered for the WRNS, and I wanted to join the boat crew. At my interview in Bristol I managed to convince the selection committee that I knew something about boats – what I didn't tell them was that I had only rowed on the River Avon for one hour!

I was posted to Plymouth for a two week training course and then on to Dartmouth. On arrival I was told to report to HMS *Raleigh*, and eventually got my instructions to crew on a motor boat which took signals and stores to various ships moored on the

Jo Hirst and crew ferrying supplies.

River Dart. After 18 months I was given my own small motor boat and attached to a mother ship which had motor torpedo-boats (MTBs) moored alongside. The MTBs would go to France to rescue resistance fighters and bring them back to the mother ship. After a couple of days resting I would take them to Kingswear station where they were escorted to London.

Unfortunately this kind of work was not available in 'civvy' street.

Any spare time we had was usually spent on the beach
Mary Haines, Pawlet

At the beginning of 1942 I volunteered to join the WRNS as a Supply Writer, and received instructions to report to Blundell Sands Hotel, in a northern suburb of Liverpool. This hotel was used as a depot for new entrants who were on probation before actually joining the service.

My two outstanding memories of this time are of scrubbing the front steps of this hotel on a cold morning with another girl who, with tears pouring down her cheeks, was singing a popular song of the time, the words being 'I haven't said thanks for that lovely weekend, those two days of heaven you helped me to spend'. Also the daily amusement of Army personnel based in a house overlooking the car park, causing the incessant rage of a male Petty Officer who was instructing us to drill and march etc.

After training I was drafted to HMS *Ferret*, Londonderry. Our living quarters was a country house on the banks of the River Foyle called Boom Hall. I believe the name originated from the days when a boom was put across the river to prevent supporters of William of Orange sailing up to Londonderry. My work was concerned with the victualling accounts of the ships based there. After a while I was transferred to the stores and with a lorry and a civilian driver delivered supplies to corvettes and destroyers who were escorting the Atlantic Convoys.

I volunteered to serve overseas and at the beginning of December 1943, after a short spell in London being kitted out with tropical uniform, and many inoculations, about 50 of us travelled by troop train to Greenock, where we went aboard the P & O liner *Strathaird*, which had been converted into a troop ship.

Eventually we docked at Bombay and for a while I worked in the victualling office, and then was transferred to Columbo, Ceylon – HMS *Larka*. Any spare time we had was usually spent on the beach. The tea planters and their wives were very kind, inviting us to spend our leave with them in the cooler atmosphere of the plantations.

Immediately after the fall of Japan, those of us off duty were asked to volunteer to help out at a hospital, as so many of the nursing staff were manning the planes flying out the very sick POWs who had been imprisoned in Changi Jail, Singapore. I shall always remember the pitiful sight of these men, living skeletons who seemed grateful for any little thing we could do to make them comfortable until professional personnel arrived to take over. I also remember how inadequate and useless I felt, as well as anger at the terrible treatment these men had undergone. Later hospital ships arrived in port bringing many, many more POWs, some of whom had worked on the infamous railways.

I returned home in a draft of about 30 Wrens on a Naval vessel that was coming back to pay off, calling at Aden, Port Said, Malta and Gibraltar, and arrived at Plymouth in July 1946, where I was released from the WRNS.

I became adept at dealing with these little white dots ...
Margo Briggs, Birkenhall

A German bomb changed the course of my life. My parents had wanted me to join the Civil Service but I had no intention of *ever* working in an office, so I went to college in the West End of London to train as a design/cutter with the ambition of working with Norman Hartnell.The bomb landed on the College annexe one night and I lost all my course work. With National Service looming and a chance I could be forced to work in a factory, I joined the WRNS.

The training school was at Mill Hill in London where we had lectures on the Naval Tradition and using Naval terms, such as 'bunk' not bed and 'galley' not kitchen. We did a lot of marching as well as learning how to scrub a floor, which we seemed to do every day. For one week I was given an alarm clock and torch so that I could rise at 5 am and wake up all the watch keepers, cooks and stewards on early duty. I hardly slept for fear the alarm would let me down.

After three weeks we were allotted our future jobs. I was to be a radar operator. This was a complete mystery to me as I'd never heard of radar, neither had three other Wrens, but we all went happily off to a Fleet Air Arm station at Ayr in Scotland for 'training'. This was a misnomer as it was an operational station and we were thrown in at the deep end.

The radar site was in a field and we lived in two Nissen huts. We discovered that radar was a tracking device and we were faced with a small green screen and told to plot little white dots – hoping they were aircraft and not flocks of seagulls! I remember the site was very cold and bleak but the Nissen huts were cosy and the cook made a wonderful lentil soup.

After a few weeks we were deemed to be trained and we were transferred to another Fleet Air Arm station at Burscough Bridge near Liverpool. Here we also lived away from the camp in a convent commandeered for Wrens at Formby. Here I drew the short straw and had to share a small room with a very large cook and her equally large and smelly dog. Cleanliness was not her top priority and the room was thick with dust. When I tried to clean it, remembering all the scrubbing at Mill Hill, I received such a tirade of foul language that I gave up.

We worked 24 hours on and 24 hours off so I picked up the habit of drinking coffee to keep awake. Again this was an operational station, plotting enemy aircraft over Liverpool. Fortunately for the residents of Liverpool, the Germans avoided it while I was there.

Luckily my problems with the cook were soon over as once again we (the original four) were moved again – this time to HMS *Kestrel* at St Merryn in Cornwall. This was bliss – most of the hotels in the area were Wrens' quarters and I lived in the Harlyn

Bay Hotel. The radar site was situated on the top of a cliff overlooking Trevorne Bay. We had a caravan for our rest periods and a rather precarious toilet hut perched at the edge of the cliff. We hardly ever went to camp so life was very free and easy. We wore 'square rig' bell bottom trousers and a square top and toured the countryside in a jeep on our 'Make and Mend Days' (rare days free from all duties).

Harlyn Bay was void of holidaymakers so we had the beach to ourselves, but we did work hard as the pilots were training and we plotted their sorties, practising bombing Gulland Rock. I became adept at dealing with these little white dots, plotting several planes at a time but the war ended and the sailors began returning home.

So the carefree life ended and I was posted to my home station – Portsmouth – and was into regular uniform with lots of marching at Whale Island, with all the rules and regulations. From there I went to Burghfield near Reading to re-muster. What did I become? A pay writer, working in an office at HMS *Condor* in Arbroath, Scotland. I loved working with figures so when I was demobbed I went to work in a bank!

We worked in the most primitive conditions
Betty Greenaway, Enmore

I couldn't wait for my 17th birthday to come, when I could apply to go into the WRNS. Six months later I was posted to, successively, Scotland, Leeds and Southampton for training, and eventually sent to work on a Fleet Air Arm squadron, training night fighter pilots and crews. With another Wren my job was supplying aircraft spares for our squadron of planes. We worked in the most primitive conditions, as the hangars we used had been bombed and were scrappily repaired, with roofing hanging dangerously. One day there was a violent storm and I saw a Mosquito aircraft lifted up and fly past our hanger, unpiloted!

Our billets were far away across the other side of the aerodrome, so we cycled to and from work, in all weathers. One day, on icy roads, I went flying off my bike, ending in a heap with my books and belongings.

Once a month we were driven in a truck to draw supplies at our parent station. We worked in a tiny office off the hangar, bitterly cold in winter, with no heating except for a one-bar fire, on which we toasted bread filched from the mess, to keep us going until the next meal (being young we were always hungry). In winter after our day's work and a long cycle back to our billet, we looked forward to a hot bath to get warm (fuel permitting), but sometimes all the pipes were frozen so with no water we couldn't even fill a hot water bottle. One cold dark evening my friend and I cycled to the nearest town hoping to find a nice fire at the WVS canteen, and a hot meal. We had the hot meal – baked beans on toast – but no fuel, so no fire, so before we faced the cold journey back to the station we curled up on the couch under our greatcoats, trying to get warm. Winters seemed to be so much colder then, but with the heavy snowfalls we all had great fun snowballing and toboganning.

I worked in P5, the code name for Bletchley Park
Patricia Mackinnon, Kingston St Mary

In August 1940 I went to a secretarial college in London, and helped at a YMCA canteen at home in Surrey in the evenings.

In 1941 I took a secretarial job with the Red Cross in the St John Wounded and Missing Department in Belgrave Square, tracing missing seamen through the International Red Cross in Geneva. I also did firewatching and canteen work. In 1943 I joined the WRNS, and after initial training I was billeted in Woburn Abbey, and worked in P5, the code-name for Bletchley Park, the code-breaking station, analysing information given us by the code breakers – particularly about the Channel Coast before D-Day.

I left the Wrens in October 1944 as I was by then married and expecting a baby.

CHAPTER 3

Auxiliary Territorial Service

The Auxiliary Territorial Service (ATS) was the women's branch of the British Army, and as such members were to be found wherever they were needed. Driving anything from motorbikes to three-ton trucks, manning nerve-centre operations rooms, controlling anti-aircraft guns, taking care of paperwork, or cooking for 500 or more men – just some of the experiences ATS girls remember. The friendliness amongst the girls and the sense of all pulling together are still vividly recalled after so many years.

My first job was in the 'Cage'
Ellen Cope, Wiveliscombe

It was July 1942 when I left home to join the ATS. I was to do my training in Guildford. As I set off with my father's little warnings ringing in my ears I felt quite excited as I had never left home before, and I was feeling very grown up.

I was at Guildford for six weeks. It was a bit hard at first, especially the square bashing; we had a Sergeant Major who could bring a sack of potatoes to attention! After our passing out parade we were all sent to various units best suited to our abilities. I wanted to go into the Royal Army Ordnance Corps (RAOC), but

was posted to the Royal Army Service Corps at Rhyl in North Wales. I was billeted in a hotel along the sea front (most hotels during the war were taken over for the forces). My job was to take care of the paperwork relating to the distribution of rations to the units in and around the Rhyl area. We worked in a huge warehouse. In November I was posted to the RAOC in Donnington (now named Telford) in Shropshire. This was certainly a very different experience, going from a hotel in Rhyl to a Nissen hut. I shared this billet with eleven other girls, all from different parts of the country: it was great, we all got on so well.

Donnington during the war was a huge garrison, completely taken over by the Army. My first job in the Ordnance Depot was in 'the cage', which stored the most valuable items. It really was a huge cage where we stayed from morning until evening. Of course we had to pack everything very carefully, and sign for everything that we handled.

About a year before D-Day I was moved from my billet in the Nissen hut to the barracks on the other side of Donnington, which were built before the war. This was sheer luxury as we had central heating, lovely bathrooms and a dining hall. All leave was cancelled as we had to prepare for D-Day. My job now was to run a section getting spares and small equipment together, which was greased and packed, then dipped in wax. It was then dropped by plane for the Resistance to pick up, so some spares were there before the D-Day landings.

The day the war ended a crowd of us visited a huge manor house where children from Dr Barnado's Home in London had been evacuated for safety. We collected as much chocolate and sweets as we could and had a lovely party with them.

Then suddenly everyone was getting demobbed and returning to 'civvy' street. Had I not got married I think I would have stayed in the ATS as I so enjoyed the friendship and everyone helping one another.

We were given a model of a vehicle made of Meccano

Emily Retallack, North Petherton

Emily Retallack.

I was born on 19th February 1923 and shortly after my 20th birthday in 1943 I received a letter from the War Office telling me to go to Taunton to the Police sports ground where I would have a medical examination prior to being called for National Service.

I was rather small at five feet two and a half inches and weighed only 7 stone 13 pounds. My parents were hoping that I would not pass the exam, and would not have to go away from home, but I passed on grade 1, and was called up for the ATS.

I was sent a travel pass to go to Wrexham, North Wales on 23rd May. There were a lot of girls on the train and on arrival at Wrexham we were picked up in a very large lorry and taken to the Royal Welsh Fusiliers camp where we were to be trained.

We were then interviewed to see what we were capable of doing. We had lectures on all kinds of trades and had to give them our choice of what we wanted to do. As I had worked in an office I chose clerical work and for second choice I decided that I would not mind a career as a driver. The clerical choice led to lots more lectures, but the driving test was more or less based on a practical mechanical test. We were given a model of a vehicle made of Meccano. When the starter bell went we had to take it to pieces. This was very easy for me as my brothers had lots of Meccano and I used to play with it when I was young. I was the first to take it apart and I had laid it out on the table in the order it had been built. When the bell went some girls had not finished taking it apart and we had to wait until it was all dismantled. We then had to put it back together as it was in the beginning.

The next few days we spent being called to the selecting board, who decided what trade we would be given. I was still wanting to do clerical, but they tried to get me to be a driver, as I was top of the test they had given us, and would have been a good mechanic. We were in training for six weeks and gradually we were posted to various units around the country.

I was posted to a REME (Royal Electrical & Mechanical Engineers) workshop in Buntingford in Hertfordshire. At first I was in an office that dealt with 'B' vehicles, that is, cars, trucks, motorbikes etc. Some months later I was transferred to the main office where I dealt with all the statistics for the War Office.

One day we were asked if any of us would volunteer to go abroad, and five of us who were all friends thought we would do this. I went on leave the following week and when I returned my best friend told me they were asked if they would go to India and that I should go to the office and change my application. In the meantime their forms had gone to the War Office and my original application was processed to go to CMF (Central Mediterranean Force). Within a short while I was on embarkation leave for ten days.

I reported to a holding unit in Bristol where I was prepared for service abroad. About three weeks later on 20th April we were taken to Liverpool dock and were embarked on the SS *Orontes*. We spent two days in the dock and during the second night the ship moved out into the bay where we stayed another night. When we woke in the morning we were off the coast of Northern Ireland.

We sailed to America in a convoy and when we were within one day's sailing of America we left the convoy and started on the route that took us to Italy. We passed Gibraltar a few days later and arrived in Naples Bay, but we were not able to dock because it was the 7th May (the day before the end of the war). We landed on the 9th May. Most of us were going to CMF headquarters in the Royal Palace in Casserta about 28 to 30 miles from Naples. The Supreme Allied Commander was Field Marshal Lord Alexander.

I first worked in the organisation office for a Major Tilney. My job was to keep the ORBAT up to date. This was the order of battle and when units moved their location they informed me by signal (like a telegram). The chief clerk lost his secretary and he asked me to work for him. His office was next to the suite of rooms where the General worked. His secretary was a Junior Commander and when she wanted to go out (when the General was out) she would ask me to sit in her office to answer the phone. It was often the War Office who were ringing.

Service life in Italy was very different from the camp that I was in, in the UK. We had very good food. When we first arrived we were working seven days a week and later we had Sunday free. We had a rest hotel in Sorrento run by the WVS and in the second year we were going there most weekends. The Army provided the transport to take us.

I was due for release in October 1946 and as there was only one other ATS girl to be repatriated we were both booked on a train from Naples. It was an ordinary train and we had a compartment on our own, and slept on the seats (one each side). When we arrived in Villach (Austria) the train did not take us any further. We were booked into a hotel for six days waiting for another train to take us to Calais. When the train arrived in Villach it was like the Orient Express. We were the only ATS on the train. The rest were officers from Casserta and the Italian wives of British soldiers who had married in Italy, and their children. We went to the dining car for our meals. When we got back to our compartment after breakfast our beds had been packed away by the train staff and after dinner in the evening on returning to our compartment our bunks were pulled down and our beds made ready. It was a lovely treat for two ATS girls.

When we arrived in London I was taken to Guildford for demob and I was there for one night going through the procedure of handing in all our kit. It was quite late in the evening when I arrived at Bridgwater station and Mum and Dad were there to meet me.

We sailed at night, unescorted and ziz-zagged across the Atlantic

Jean Pegler, Wiveliscombe

I was called up for duty with the ATS on 3rd September 1939, and served until I was discharged on compassionate grounds in spring 1946, as I was pregnant. I served in this country mainly, on the administration side of the ATS, but in April 1945 I was given a posting to Canada to exchange duties with a Canadian Women's Army Corps (CWAC) officer for three months.

I was a Junior Commander (Captain) at the time and joined 15 other ATS officers of similar rank, on 10th April, to embark for Canada. We sailed at night, unescorted, and zig-zagged across the Atlantic, expecting to be torpedoed any minute. The ship was crowded with troops, and six of us were berthed in a cabin meant for two; we had to dress and undress two at a time as there was so little space.

We berthed in New Brunswick, where we were given a super meal before taking a train to Montreal, from there we (I had two other ATS officers with me at the start) were dropped off at destinations en route. I had been posted to Calgary and the journey took five days on the train. We had comfortable berths, super food and we were waited on hand and foot. When we left Montreal it was warm like a summer's day in England, but when we got to Calgary, Alberta, there was over a foot of snow! I was posted to Currie Barracks, a regular Army barracks, and had my first real taste of central heating. The huts the CWAC lived in were so warm everyone wore light summer uniforms inside, but it was a very different story outside.

I consider the ATS had the best out of this exchange; we left behind war torn Britain and came to a land of plenty. Many times whilst in Canada when it came to paying the bill at a cafe etc, I was told at the desk that it had been paid by a member of the public eating there. I did very little army work but talked to various groups about the conditions in England. I put on a tray one person's rations for a week, and when I showed the tray to illustrate my lecture half the audience didn't believe me, and when you saw the meals we ate in the officers' mess you could understand why – beef steaks that hung over the sides of the plate, and unlimited butter and cream! It was with regret we boarded a ship to return to England after such a lovely break, but we thought there were a few Canadians who knew a little more about war torn Britain after our visit.

Jeeps were wonderful to drive, like toys!
Gwen Clark, Otterford & Bishopswood

In 1943 I was 17, old enough to volunteer for the forces. I was working as a secretary, but wanted to drive, anything! It was difficult to get petrol then, and I had only had a few tentative lessons on the local taxi.

I joined the ATS (Auxiliary Territorial Service) against the wishes of everyone I knew – why didn't I go for the WRNS or the WAAF? I stuck to my guns and went through the initial training in North Wales for three weeks. I put in for a driving course, and was sent to a holding unit in Devon for another three weeks, enjoying the summer sunshine on countless route marches, as they didn't really know what to do with us. From there I was posted back to North Wales (about three miles from the previous camp) for a ten-week driving course. My ambition was getting there! We were kitted out with trousers, battledress, boots, leather jerkins, leather driving gloves, overalls and kerchiefs, and had the privilege given to all drivers to wear the strap of our hat across the top instead of the usual place. This was an odd privilege, I don't know the origin of it, but I do know we jealously guarded our right. The trousers were a bit of a letdown in the first few weeks as the stores had run out of them, and we were issued with breeches and knee length puttees temporarily, which were dreadful to put on in a hurry in the mornings, and we all felt pretty silly in them. Eventually we got our trousers!

My first encounter with an Army truck was a three-ton Fordson, large and imposing to us. Three of us went with the instructor, who asked if anyone had had any driving experience. Of course, Muggins had to say I had a little, so she said, 'Right, up you go and let's see what you can do.' Um. I clambered into the driving seat and found the controls. I had done some double de-clutching on private cars but these huge pedals and very large gear lever took a bit of getting used to, not to speak of the crash gearbox, which had to be timed exactly to the speed of the engine or it just wouldn't go in. 'Change down before you go down,' the instructor said. Oh, yes, the wretched gear would not engage, and

Gwen Clark and friends.

I was left with a three-tonner hurtling down the slope in neutral with a startled instructor and two terrified companions in the back. Luckily for me the braking system was extremely efficient, but from then onwards I had a wholesome respect for all the various gearboxes we encountered.

Our instructor gave us one piece of advice which I always remembered – 'Always expect an elephant in the middle of the road round a blind corner!' It was good advice, which I eventually passed on to my son who is an articulated lorry driver, and he told me the other day that he still keeps it in mind!

We alternated our driving lessons with workshop sessions, which were great. We dismantled and put together most parts of vehicles, and learned what was going on under the bonnet.

At the end of the course we took our driving test – mine was through Chester, a lovely city, in an Army ambulance (Katy). They were great to drive, but had not much lock, so my reversing could have been better! Anyway, I passed, and was then asked which branch I wanted to belong to – ambulance driving, staff driving or convoy work. Most of the girls settled for staff driving on my course, but I wanted to do convoys, as it meant trucks rather than cars. A couple of us were posted to a Vehicle Reserve Depot (VRD) near Darlington, Durham, and then went on leave to tell our families all about it.

The VRD was a fascinating place. Situated in the grounds of a stately castle, with a live-in family, two lakes, spacious grounds and woods, and two herds of deer, we must have been a great trial to the owners. We filled the beautiful woods with over 2,000 trucks of all sizes, tucked away beneath the trees for camouflage, built rows of Nissen huts for offices and living quarters, used the ancient stables for battery stores etc., and in general created mayhem, but all in a very good cause. I was in a hut with 13 other girls, all drivers, as our hours were different from the rest of the camp. There were mostly drivers, of course, with cooks and office staff to keep us going. We had a REME base workshop to keep the trucks running, and Depot Transport to transport drivers to or from the railway station at Darlington, as we travelled equally far by train going to or from the convoy points.

I was put onto the 15 cwt bay, as we always had one month convoy and one month on our bay. This took away the strain of constant driving, and kept up the maintenance and parking of the bays. We learned to park in long exact lines, take off batteries, drain water, and generally get them ready for a long stay. When they were required, we had to reverse the procedure, batteries on, fill up whatever was needed, and the biggest struggle of all, tow them out from their places where they had invariably bogged down in the mud. For this job we had a Guy gun quad, my favourite vehicle, fully armoured, with many gears and a very reliable winch. This managed to get the most recalcitrant truck unstuck. We also had to check for birds' nests under the bonnets, and had to gently remove them to the nearest place hoping that the mother would find them. I learned to love the countryside in those woods, with pheasants, woodpeckers and numerous types of birds, and a wealth of wild flowers.

When my first convoy month came along, I first of all had a short local run with another driver to get me into the swing of things. The second one was a bit more serious. About thirty small Utility trucks (affectionately known as Tillies) had to go to the docks at Glasgow in a hurry, and did we hurry! I hadn't yet learnt the extremely odd fact that while the front car may be doing a gentle 25 mph, the rear ones were tearing along at 50 or 60 to keep up. This was a favourite place, but as I had just emerged from training camp where we did a sedate 30 mph everywhere, finding myself at the back of this one was a bit hair-raising. After an exhilarating trip we reached Glasgow, and not knowing where on earth I was going I did my best to stay with the crowd amongst traffic and trams. Fine until my wheels became channelled in the tramlines with trams bearing down in both directions. After an embarrassing struggle I freed the Tilly, only to find that the convoy had disappeared out of sight! What a relief when I eventually found the docks and the rest of the convoy!

These convoys recall a kaleidoscope of memories – driving for hours in sunshine, rain, snow, ice, thick fog – always travelling steadily to our destination, the regulation 25 yards apart (except when we got split up in large cities and got hopelessly lost!). We had no signposts, and only the leader had written instructions, although we all knew where we were going, and our instinct seemed to lock in to prevent any real problems – and even now I am rarely lost on roads (especially with the numerous signposts we now have!).

We did drive at night, especially in wintertime. And as the rear light was one tiny red dot, the big differential under the truck was painted white with a light shining on to it, better for not being seen by aircraft and much better for our eyesight – a small red light tends eventually to come and go and send you batty.

One completely all-night trip nearly had disastrous consequences for me – we had taken a lot of Bedford three tonners to Liverpool, stopping at Preston overnight. One of the trucks broke down so we left it at Preston, only to find on arriving at Liverpool that the ship was leaving that night. Three of us drove back to collect the stray, which had by then been repaired, then drove once again to the docks. We had another lot of vehicles to

Jeeps were fun.

take back with us, so went straight on the next day, making us three having driven all one day, all one night and all the next day. Needless to say on the way home I fell asleep and awoke bumping across the grass on the opposite verge. All was well, and I learnt to stay awake in future. On one trip a male driver fell asleep and drove through two hedges and a field before waking up!

We always had plenty of rest stops – we knew all the transport cafes on the North/South run, and all the spots which could take a large number of vehicles at the same time. We had to have 'penny stops', impossible in towns with so many to park, so we would stop on a suitable country road with a good hedge and gate. Later in the war when we had male drivers among us, the order came 'girls to the left, men to the right', and we had to find a hedge on both sides!

We had some very old trucks, First World War vintage, with no windscreens or side windows, just canvas flaps, the front ones tying under your chin. Fine in the warm weather but in the winter we could be heading into freezing snow, with icicles on our eyebrows. There was, of course, no heating in any of the trucks, and at the end of each day the radiators had to be drained, and refilled early the next morning – very cold on the fingers.

It was a lovely free life, away from the rigours and discipline of the camp. We had one person in charge of each convoy, plus if we were lucky a driver-mechanic. I went on a driver-mech course, which was very enjoyable, and so qualified for this, though as most of the vehicles were pretty new I wasn't called upon too often. The 'repairs on the road' time came after the war, when all the old, worn out, decrepit vehicles were taken down south to be broken up. These convoys were hilarious, and always accompanied by a team of REME engineers. They would select, say, 20 vehicles, get ten of them just running, and they would tow the other ten. As you can imagine, these were the longest lasting convoys of all as there was always one or another truck breaking down. I finished up once (in another three ton Fordson) travelling with a large petrol tank tied on the roof of the cab, fixed up to supply the engine with fuel by gravity as the fuel pump refused to work. I think it would be slightly illegal today, but it did get me there.

Sometimes, we would be haring along to catch a ship leaving port, or just ambling back from the works with brand new vehicles ready to be stored in the VRD until needed. Some would stay a year or so, some a few weeks, depending on which theatre of war needed them. We had sand-yellow painted ones for desert warfare, occasionally white-tracked little ones for Russia, Canadian Chevs and Fords, hefty American Dodges and Studebakers, and of course the beloved Jeeps, all in dull khaki with no extra camouflage. They all without exception had masked lights, and sometimes when boarding a ship the lights would be covered with sacking, as if they were stored on deck it stopped reflections.

Jeeps were wonderful to drive, like toys. I and a friend were privileged one Christmas to deliver two amphibious jeeps to Ipswich. These were most unusual to look at and wherever we stopped a crowd would gather round to examine them.

My most momentous convoy was with jeeps, on 6th June 1944. We drove to Southampton, not to the docks, but to line them with thousands of other trucks filling all the roads. We had not realised the impact of this until we arrived, and were wondering why we were plied with numerous cups of tea en route! It was an impressive and proud day.

We learnt a lot about life
Irene Hooper, North Petherton

I worked for the Tone Vale Shirt and Collar factory at Bridgwater, but in 1941, when I was 20, I joined the ATS. At first I learnt about marching etc, at Honiton in Devon, then moved on to Herefordshire to learn how to drive. I then came to Blandford camp where I lived in wooden barracks.

We sometimes took American soldiers to Musgrove Park Hospital, the first part of which was built by the Americans. We took them in cars until they had their own ambulances to transport them. I became a Lance Corporal while at Blandford as I was good at working out how many miles per gallon each vehicle did. I drove cars and ambulances, not motorbikes as I could not kick start motorbikes as a result of an injury from falling out of the back of an ambulance.

After a camp in Dorset, I was billeted in a hotel on the front at Weymouth and I was there for D-Day. We drove some of the English and American officers up to the top of a hill to watch the crossing. I then drove a 30-cwt lorry to Southampton to pick up army personnel.

After that I went on several courses in different locations, ending up at Winchester where I became a L/Sgt. Mechanic, and did repairs on various vehicles. To me it was a lovely life in the ATS, although it was wartime – we learnt a lot about life, which we hadn't known about. After demob I returned to my old job, but it was difficult getting used to working with only girls again.

We did our turn as fire pickets
Eileen Rogerson, Puriton

In September 1941 I joined the ATS and after a month at Wrexham doing basic training and then a month at Chester doing a signals course I was posted to Brompton Road, London.

There we took over from the men who had manned the Gun Operation Room. This was the nerve centre for the Gun and Balloon Sites around London. We worked in the disused Brompton Road underground station and our job involved manning the switchboards, teleprinters and plotting. The plots came from Uxbridge RAF station and were then relayed to the guns. We also plotted where rockets and doodlebugs fell.

One night a girl actually plotted a rocket which landed on her home in the East End. She was, of course, sent on leave but she did come back and told us that her little sister had been killed and the whole house demolished.

We did our turn as fire pickets and during a raid one night we were on the roof (which was flat) armed with stirrup pumps and buckets of sand. I must say that the sight was quite amazing. The search lights were sweeping the incoming planes and the guns were firing, sending up puffs of smoke. The General was not happy. His

ATS girls marching with a swing.

language was quite colourful. When he saw us he yelled, 'Get those ****** ATS out of here' – we were only doing our duty!

I stayed with the same crowd that I started with. We were great mates and I am still in touch with some of them. About a month before D-Day a small contingent of Royal Artillery joined us – all very hush hush. When they departed suddenly we knew something was happening. One of this group became my husband in 1945!

We all got excited when the Italians capitulated and then when VE Day came we were stood down and we made our way to the Mall and joined the crowd which swept us along to Buckingham Palace where the King, Queen and the Princesses came out on the balcony. It really was very exciting, everyone joining hands, singing and dancing.

Life was a bit flat after that. When VJ Day came I was given a stripe, which I really didn't want! I was then posted to an Education Unit at Royston. At last my demob number came up and I found myself at Paddington station at 11 pm. I arrived at Taunton in the early hours and was taken to Norton Barracks where I handed in my uniform and was given about £5 to buy civilian clothes. A brief handshake from the CO and good wishes etc, and I was once more a civilian!

We were machine gunned every morning
Jean Grundy, Keinton Manderville

It was in September 1942 that I decided that factory life was not for me. I chose the services and joined the ATS. My initial training was at Glen Parva Barracks in Leicester and then at Arborfield in Berkshire where I was trained as a telephonist for a gun site. Here I spent most of my duty time underground at the command post where we plotted the enemy planes coming in: not a glamorous life, but certainly active!

I had 26 moves in my three years in the forces and though each one had its drama and a tale to tell, I will select the most memorable.

I was later trained on radar, and when the rockets and doodlebugs attacked (very frightening), the British Mark 1 & 2 Radar became obsolete and we had to be trained quickly on the Canadian 584. I really was like a 'cat with nine lives' with so many narrow escapes. On the East Coast we were machine-gunned every morning by very low flying aircraft – we just dropped to the floor and hoped for the best. When in Plymouth there was a direct hit on the YWCA where I would have been if I hadn't caught the last ferry from Torpoint to Millbrook. When in London at Golders Green, three of us had an evening pass; I wanted to go to a NAAFI dance, but the others wanted to go to the Stage Door Canteen. It was two votes to one and we missed the dance. That night there was a direct hit on the NAAFI and there were no survivors.

On D-Day we were at Millbrook where we were 'prisoners' for three weeks carrying out secret work. We were allowed no contact with the outside world, no letters home and everyone was confined to camp. For three days and nights, troops, tanks and other vehicles passed by the camp, as well as thousands of soldiers, including many Americans stationed at Treganthe who threw cigarettes and chocolates over the camp hedge. We knew something big was going on – but didn't know what.

We were eventually taken off active service and trained as office staff. I ended my army days at Aldershot isolation hospital – a very sad time for me. Ambulances brought young soldiers off the troop ships from Southampton, mainly terminally ill with CSM, smallpox, typhoid or war wounds. Upset parents would arrive to collect the personal belongings of their dead sons.

I was granted a fortnight's unpaid leave in September 1945 to go home to be married, but I had to return until being demobbed on 26th October. I went back to my home village on the ridge of the Malvern Hills where I used my wartime skills only in clerical work as I joined my husband in running a family grocery business until retirement in 1980. No more air raids, thank God.

I had to get up at 4 am to cook breakfast
Edith Thirkell, Kingston St Mary

I volunteered for the ATS and enlisted on 2nd September 1941 – W/78373: that number I have never forgotten in spite of a poor memory in those days. I went by train to Honiton and met other girls all carrying their gas masks in little cardboard boxes. We were met at the station to be escorted to Honiton Camp, originally home to the Devonshire Regiment. We walked that mile in twos and the Sergeant Major took us into the camp to the Quarter Master's Store to collect all our requirements including bedding. We were measured for our uniform and then marched across the camp with all the kit and told we were responsible for paying for its replacement, even down to our cutlery.

I was in training there for nine weeks learning how to cook, as my eyesight would not pass the test for driving which I would have liked. Although later I was cooking for 500 to 600 troops who were convalescent, either to be invalided out of the army or returning to fight again. People were very kind and I had lots of lifts. If it was a Saturday and I could reach the garage at one end of Honiton a large white lorry would take me to Taunton. I saved

Members of the ATS on early morning parade.

all my cigarette coupons for the driver. I always went back by train as we had to be in by a certain time and report to the guard at the barrack gate. If I had a weekend pass I would go to Kingston St Mary church for the 11 am service as I had been in the choir before the war and would sometimes sit in the choir beside Margaret Broomfield in her WAAF uniform, daughter of our village blacksmith and he would be in the choir as well.

I was posted to Sherford Camp in Taunton, where there were two cookhouses catering for up to 600 men. If you were a duty cook you had to get up at 4 am to cook breakfast for men catching trains. We did finish work earlier in those days and were then free to be off duty. I used to set off hitch hiking for home in Kingston St Mary at Bobbets opposite our post office.

Towards the end of the war the whole convalescent camp moved from Sherford to the east of the country and because I had a compassionate posting in the first place due to my mother's high blood pressure and being the only child, I got out of it and was sent to Rowford Lodge at Cheddon Fitzpaine to the officers' mess, and was discharged from there on 17th December 1945. Although it was great to know the war was ended I could not help feeling sorry at saying goodbye and I still write to several of my friends at Christmas. After preparing meals all morning and then standing on a box at the hot plate serving 500 men or more I had been tired but felt the job was worth doing.

CHAPTER 4

—◦◦◦—

Nursing

—◦◦◦—

N ursing had always been a career open to women but the war brought in many new recruits, some undertaking traditional training as student or pupil nurses, while others became involved as nursery nurses or through the Red Cross, St John Ambulance Brigade or Voluntary Aid Detachment (VAD). VADs were unqualified, but provided essential first aid and general nursing care both at home and abroad. Nurses, obviously, were faced with the very worst that war brings and they had to be disciplined and resilient to cope with the sorrow and horror of nursing terribly injured soldiers, prisoners of war and civilians. Their resourcefulness and dedication, particularly when far from home, cannot be forgotten.

—◦◦◦—

The teamwork was wonderful
Margaret Thorndike, Anstey

When the war broke out I joined the Land Army and went to Seale Hayne College, where I learned how to milk cows, look after pigs, drive a tractor, and plough a field with two horses. We had great fun.

I then went to work on a farm about three miles from Bognor in Sussex. I lived with the cowman and his wife. Work started at 5 am and a large herd was milked by hand, three times a day. The evening milking was not much fun as it was in the dark, no lights, and bombers droning overhead. I had one weekend off a month, and after an exciting train journey with more bombers trying to bomb the line, I went home.

I enjoyed it, but after a year I thought I should do something with a future, so I enrolled as a nurse at University College Hospital. Discipline was very strict and we worked very hard. Although we had to be in by 10 pm nobody thought to stop us going on the flat roof of the nurses' home in the middle of the night to watch the bombs come down. Actually the police were very helpful at getting us in the windows after 10 o'clock!

Three days before D-Day we were sent to Chertsey, to a casualty clearing station. This consisted of about 20 army units in the grounds of a large mansion. We had to make beds and prepare everything for convoys of wounded men coming over from France. Convoys of about 200 arrived, usually in the middle of the night. They usually stayed two or three days and were then sorted out and sent to permanent army hospitals. The theatre worked non-stop and the more serious cases were kept longer. Our final exam results came through, but the celebrations were cut short by the arrival of another convoy.

The teamwork was wonderful – concerts were arranged and the doctors (mostly from St Thomas's) got up a band and played to the men, and the whole thing was exciting and interesting. Penicillin was just coming into its own and by the time we had given four-hourly injections to 20 men we became very good at it.

Altogether I enjoyed every minute.

We worked from 9 at night to 9 in the morning
Penny Harrison, East Chinnock

At the outbreak of war I was still in the last year of grammar school, but as all exams that year were cancelled, I left. I went to work in London in the accounts department of Moyses Stevens, the Court Florist. During this time I was in the St John Ambulance Brigade – working in St George's Hospital two or three evenings a week, and MayDay Hospital near my home at weekends.

After a while I volunteered to be with the Voluntary Aid Detachment (VAD) in the Navy. I was posted to a hospital in Barrow Gurney – just outside Clevedon in Somerset. This was very hard work with a shortness of nurses and many sailors and marines to care for. We worked sometimes from 9 at night to 9 in the morning for a month without a break, then we had three days 'stand off'. We then did sometimes mornings or sometimes afternoons. During this time we had to attend lessons and take exams. After one of the exams I was considered 'good enough' to be sent to a laboratory in Clevedon where the first batch ever of penicillin was made. I would rather have stayed on the wards – but one didn't argue with the Navy.

The First Aid Post was at the town hall
Nora Smith, Appley Cross

A year before the Second World War began I attended a lecture about the Red Cross at a local hospital in Chatham, Kent. I therefore joined the St John Ambulance Brigade, and I also became a member of the ARP. Our first aid post was formed at a school near the town hall, though later it was moved to the town hall itself. I passed the first aid exam and worked full time on twelve-hourly shifts. At first when the siren sounded denoting an air raid we all ran to the first aid post and stayed there until the all clear sounded, but later if we were off duty we didn't have to report to the first aid post.

Later when the raids lessened in Chatham I was seconded to work at Shorts Aircraft factory, making screws and small metal objects for planes. I worked there until I had permission to join my husband abroad.

NURSING

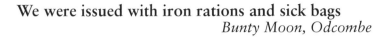

We were issued with iron rations and sick bags
Bunty Moon, Odcombe

In 1939 I joined the Red Cross Bank detachment and, taking a number of their simple tests including one on gas, I started going to University College Hospital to work on the wards in the evenings. This inspired me to see if I could train as a nurse. Had I left this decision much longer I would probably have been detailed to stay in the banking service.

I was accepted by the Matron, Mrs Jackson, and on 6th May 1940, I, with all my worldly possessions, reported to the hospital. I had to equip myself with the hospital uniform, and buy my own textbooks. The salary for the first year was £20, rising to £24 in the second year. This did not matter too much because as the bombing began and the Battle of Britain was raging there was nothing much to spend money on.

The first six weeks were spent in the nurses' training school, a fairly new institute. I knew that I had to work hard, as I had only myself to depend on and if I failed the tests, I would be out.

My first ward was a women's medical under a dragon of a sister called Polly and I fell foul of her when I blew the whistle about an ex-patient who kept coming to the ward to pinch the patients' rations. I was horrified when all of the other nurses who obviously knew what was going on denied any knowledge. Shortly after this I was put on night duty. Bombs were falling and shrapnel was bouncing off the roof at night. Patients, when well enough, were sent out to Ashridge House in Hertfordshire, where the Conservative Country House had been taken over and huts for wards were constructed in the grounds. We nurses all had to do a spell there, I think I must have been there for about six months.

On my first night duty we worked twelve hours a night with half an hour off for a meal and one night off a fortnight. Later we got two nights off. Sleeping in the day was very difficult and I existed on about four hours which was all I could manage.

One day while we were serving lunch at Ashridge, a lone German bomber flew over the hospital and deposited a number of bombs but, very fortunately, they all fell into the soft ground and did no damage, but things could have been very different. Back at the UCH main hospital the bombing had got worse, and incendiary bombs were also being used.

I have one or two memories of that time. One night we were ringed by fires. London University and Maples in Tottenham Court Road were blazing. We had to prepare to accept patients from other parts of the hospital, but the bombers did not manage to set us alight.

Another time, a large Winchester bottle of liquid paraffin was blown off the window ledge and shattered all over a composition floor. My job was to clean it up. No detergent then – newspaper, soap and water – ugh! One night after a bomb had shattered gas mains supplying the hospital I had to prepare the patients' breakfasts. We had electric lighting and steam sterilizers. So ingenuity was required. I cooked porridge, scrambled dried egg and tea in the sterilizer!

I had managed to do quite well in all the tests, much better than anything I had managed at school. We took our finals in 1943 which I passed, but had to do one more year to obtain a hospital certificate. During that year I applied to the Queen Alexandra Imperial Nursing Service – the army nurses, and was accepted to await call up. Soon after D-Day I was to report to Oxford and was billeted in Lincoln College with the new intake. Here we were fitted with our uniform – khaki, as the traditional red and grey of the QANS was suspended.

Our first job in the army was to nurse D-Day casualties in the Oxford Examination Halls. Most of the patients were badly wounded.

A few weeks later posting came for our group to proceed to Watford, where we were billeted in a school, but no nursing was carried on there. It was very hot and we slept out in the open until we were told that we might be hit by shrapnel and should stay under cover.

August 1944: After a week or two further orders came. We were to proceed by train to …, which turned out to be Eastleigh in Hampshire, to a tented enclosed overnight transit camp, where we were prepared for the Channel crossing. We were issued with iron rations and sick bags. The iron rations also contained six sheets of toilet paper! In the morning we boarded buses to take us to

Southampton docks, where a hospital ship awaited us. It was a lovely sight after all the grey and dun coloured vehicles which of necessity were camouflaged. It was gleaming white interspersed with pale green.

We boarded for what turned out to be an exceedingly rough crossing. There were no ports on the French mainland freed from the Germans and we had to stay overnight on board. In the morning we had to jump off the ship into a naval amphibious craft (DUKW) to be ferried to a jetty at Corseilles in Normandy.

The German line was around Falaise in Normandy by then and most of the serious casualties were being sent back to the UK. We were taken to 101 British General Hospital outside Bayeux. It was a tented hospital based around a chateau. There was a huge Red Cross laid out on the ground at the entrance. Conditions were rather primitive. Drinking water was brought round in a tanker, food was adequate but monotonous: soya sausages, beans etc, and tea made with a concoction of dried milk and sugar. I remember that cider was served with our lunch which always made me sleepy in the afternoon. No clothes washing facilities and we could queue for an occasional bath in the village where a French woman heated water by using wood and twigs. Men and women would be sitting in the courtyard waiting their turn.

Drying clothes was also a problem and I can remember taking one or two articles to bed with me hoping that my body warmth would do the trick, and waking in the night having dreamt that I was lying on a marble slab.

Nursing was very light, some minor casualties, but mainly medical sick, self inflicted wounds and some German POWs.

November 1944: Orders came for the hospital to be packed up and with a group of others we were taken to Arramanches to board a ship over the remains of the Mulberry Harbour, the miracle construction which was towed across the channel on D-Day to provide a port on the French coast. By then a severe gale had damaged it but we were still able to travel on it to get to the boat. We were taken to Goodwood House in Sussex where we stayed until January. Further orders sent us to Tilbury where we again boarded a boat for Belgium. As we approached the coast we could hear gunfire from Dunkirk which still contained an enclave of Germans. We landed at Ostend where we saw the huge sand ramparts, constructed by German slave labour.

At Ecloo, a little town halfway between Bruges and Ghent, we were billeted in a convent. It was a busy time as the Germans were trying to break through in the Ardennes, known as the Battle of the Bulge. I can remember a ward of badly wounded soldiers and my job was to go round giving penicillin injections every three hours using a syringe and needle which had to be boiled up after each patient on a spirit stove. Penicillin was in its infancy and there were quite a lot of allergic reactions. We were acting as a transit stop for the men being taken back to the UK.

The war in Europe looked as if it was coming to an end and I did what everybody said you should not do in the army and that was to volunteer for a posting to the East. It was accepted and I was posted back to the UK and then on to Shaftesbury in Wiltshire, where we were nursing local troops. Here I, and a small group of nurses got ourselves kitted up for the tropics – khaki drill etc.

The posting came through and our group travelled to Liverpool where we boarded a troop ship. We were three weeks at sea passing through the Mediterranean which by then had been freed of German and Italian troops, and down the Red Sea arriving in Bombay, where we then travelled to Poona, a peace time military station. This was a transit camp where all our inoculations were repeated. We were asked to put down our names to state our preference of where we would like to serve, with no guarantees given. I put down Burma and was posted to the Royal West African Frontier Force (RWAFF) in Chittagong on the Indo/Burma frontier in Assam, but never got there because when the six of us reached Calcutta we were told by the RTO (Rail Transport Officer) that the RWAFF were being transferred to the Madras region in southern India.

By then the A-bombs had been dropped and the Japanese surrendered – in fact that happened while we were still in Poona and I remember a wow of a party to celebrate. After about a week staying in the Grand Hotel, Calcutta, then a temporary transit camp, we boarded a train for Madras – an overnight journey from north to south of India. We arrived in Madras at about 8 pm and were told by the RTO that only a small detachment of the RWAFF had so far arrived.

The RTO did not know what to do with six nursing sisters at that time of night so he arranged for us to travel to some place where there was a small RAF unit. We were 'pennies from heaven' when we arrived and I can remember six of us being raced round the airfield in the middle of the night. The rest of the night was spent looking after one of our number who was very drunk.

The next morning some of the officers from the RWAFF detachment arrived to collect us. Mandapallee was some distance away and when we got there we were put in to the 'bashers' (straw type huts) vacated for our benefit by the officers. We were only there for a week or two and one of our number was killed in a road accident when the jeep she was travelling in veered off the dirt road.

We were ordered to re-cross India to a place on the West Coast where there was a large camp of West Africans awaiting repatriation. It was a very restless camp as they were all anxious to return to Africa and some of them were becoming a menace. In fact nurses' quarters had to be guarded by European troops, and I believe there was some sort of scare.

While I was there I contracted malaria and was hospitalised. Shortly after, I was discharged from hospital and orders came for us to return to Mandapallee as the RWAFF had arrived there.

We boarded the train and about 4 pm it arrived at a station in the back of beyond and we were told that we would not be going on until 8 in the morning. There was a rest house available in the area, but as the station was teeming with Indians who slept all night on the platform we decided to stay with our kit and sleep in the waiting room. There were monkeys everywhere and they made short work of any food we were carrying. In the middle of the night we all woke up to sit scratching ourselves as the monkeys had made their contribution. Next morning we carried on with the journey and arrived eventually at Mandapallee, a tented camp.

After a period an order came through for another nurse and myself to be seconded to Avadi, part of a huge camp being set up to invade Burma, but which now was not necessary. We were posted to the African ward of an Indian British General hospital.

My colleague and I did not do much nursing as the African orderlies did all that was needed. The patients were not generally very ill, just the usual run of medical ailments. I did not like it there – my colleague and I did not get on together and the MO appointed to the ward was 'wet'.

One thing happened there. I was called by the orderly to see an African, who had been in for about a week very ill but undiagnosed – one suggestion had been that he had been cursed or some such thing by the witch doctor. However, the patient was then appearing slightly more alert. When I examined him I noticed he had large blobs on his extremities and this rang a bell in my head – smallpox – which it was. No one else contracted it, fortunately. He was isolated with two orderlies to care for him and his bedding was put out in the sun to kill the bugs.

Thrown into the deep end at Bristol Royal Infirmary
Olive Maggs, Bradford-on-Tone

Olive Maggs with her sister.

I was 17 years old when the war started in 1939. My sister had gone into the Women's Auxiliary Air Force (WAAF) but I decided to do nursing as in that situation I would probably not be sent so far from home. As our mother was a widow we did not want both of us to be too far away – we lived in Bristol.

First of all I had two weeks' training at the Bristol Royal Infirmary – then straight onto a male ward of about 50 beds! Quite a shock at first but I think we soon became quite efficient – you jolly well had to.

Next I was sent to an orthopaedic hospital outside Bristol. There was a jolly time with soldiers who were having knee operations etc. This was in 1942.

I then went back to Bristol to the Eye Hospital as I had decided to do a full two-year training. I enjoyed my time there except that once a week, or so it seemed, we had rabbit stew! We were also forced by Matron to drink a whole glass of milk with our lunch every day. At the end of the two years, in 1944, I was married – can you guess? – to a doctor. D-Day was just after our wedding so we could not go far away for our honeymoon as all the doctors had to be available to come on duty when the invasion of France took place.

Before becoming a nurse I had been an Air Raid Warden in my home area. Fortunately the nearest bombs were dropped in nearby fields so you could say that I was one of the lucky ones.

It was not all work and no play
Betty Hayes, Cranmore and Doulting

I left school in 1940 to go to work at the children's hospital in Gloucester, now no longer in use. We had three hours off a day, half a day off per week, and one day off a month. We were paid £12 per annum, minus National Insurance. The worst part was having to stop parents from visiting their children, which is what happened then.

After two years, at the age of 18, I went to do my general training at St John's Hospital, Lewisham, which is now demolished. I arrived to find an enormous hole where a land mine had landed. My pay went up to £30 per annum, I think, with one day off a week, three hours a day, and four hours on Sunday.

After three months I was transferred to the British Legion Emergency Hospital near Maidstone. The wards were long, with 40 beds to a ward. There I saw malaria, colitis, soldiers with leg amputations, and sometimes we had a ward full of patients suffering from the effects of smallpox vaccinations.

One man who sticks out in my memory had seen his two sons killed in front of him. He wouldn't eat and withdrew into himself. Obviously, he was suffering from depression, but the doctor put him in 'jankers' (punishment) and he used to be marched up and down the aisles separating the wards.

It was not all work and no play there. We often went to dances in Maidstone, West Malling and Ashford barracks, as girls were in short supply!

After nine months I was transferred back to Lewisham where the food was considerably better, along with the living accommodation, although the rules were much stricter. Whilst there I have fond memories of listening to Glenn Miller and his dance orchestra. I even danced to his music live. I danced at several palais, and was introduced to the ballet, which I loved.

Before D-Day I was told by Matron to be prepared to go overseas. I had to get a blanket from home, and we would be issued with a kidney dish and instruments. We didn't go to France as it happens, there were not as many soldiers wounded as envisaged, though many more were killed.

Not long afterwards the V1 flying bombs, or doodlebugs as we called them, started. The nurses upstairs came down to us, as they thought it was safer. Some slept on the floor and others shared beds with us. Matron came in and she was horrified. We knew nothing about lesbianism then, besides I had always slept with my sister, as had other nurses. After that we had to sleep in the air raid shelter.

All the waiting list patients' operations were cancelled and we concentrated on air raid casualties. The casualties were operated on and shipped to other hospitals in the country by converted Green Line coaches, holding about seven beds. We were given a list of hospitals in places we passed through if we needed help. After the doodlebugs came the V2 rockets. We had started doing ordinary operations again by then. I was transferred to theatre work. After the daytime operations we had to wash the walls ready for the casualties. At one time we had two operating tables in one theatre, with three surgeons operating on one patient; one for the head, one for the trunk and one for the lower limbs. I well remember one morning going outside about 7 am having started at 7.30 am the previous day, to see a most spectacular sunrise. We went to bed in the shelter, but were woken up at 10.30 to go on duty. We had been working so hard that Matron gave us one and a half days off.

Eventually things quietened down and VE Day arrived. Matron said we could go up to London after finishing work at 9 pm. Crowds of people lined The Mall up to Buckingham Palace. Winston Churchill came on the balcony. We all shouted for the King and his family to come out on the balcony, which of course they did. I also heard a trumpet playing and afterwards realised it was Humphrey Lyttleton. I think some of the buildings were floodlit – what a marvellous night – I had never seen anything like it before.

A 'Blitz tested' nurse in India
Barbara Braund, Batcombe

July 18th 1944: We sailed from Greenock in the *Strathaver*; a troop ship run by officers of the RAF, or rather administered by the RAF. We had mustered for a week in Baker Street and there were 250 of us. It took nearly a month to get to Bombay and on arrival, we were put on a hospital train. *Pathe Gazette* was also on the platform to take our arrival pictures. 'Blitz tested' nurses they called us. There is no doubt that we were used for Indian propaganda: the country is so large that many people did not realise that Japan had already invaded parts of the North East, so we were fussed over considerably.

Our first stop was Kirkee, a huge regimental depot where we disembarked and were taken to a transit camp. We started work on the wards the next day. The BGH (British General Hospital) was a large general hospital – the sort that was built alongside huge army depots. Here we nursed all the diseases we had read about in our tropical nursing books – mostly malaria, typhoid and dysentery. Sharing the nursing were Italian POWs, presumably sent out to camps in India due to a shortage of space in Great Britain.

In early September we mustered in front of the Mess to meet the Principal Matron. As she walked down our ranks, dear Miss

Corsair, our Red Cross officer, kept telling her that this lot are going to Bangalore, this lot are going to Calcutta and these few girls are staying here. She was squashed flat by the Principal Matron who turned on her and said, 'Not at all, these girls are moving up to the front.' We were delighted. More tropical gear was issued including a canvas wash basin, bed and bath. By this time we had abandoned the white velour hat issued to us by the Red Cross (I should say, purchased by us from Scotts for about £4), also our pith helmets. Later we were given BORs, khaki uniform until we could get our trousers and shirts run up in the Indian bazaar. So out went the useless skirt and top which was the uniform chosen for best and in came cotton trousers and bush jackets.

It took us nearly four days to reach our final destination, which was Assam. We stopped overnight at the Grand Hotel in Calcutta – a sort of transit hotel where there were endless comings and goings. We were very popular and had a wonderful evening except for the bugs living in the wicker chairs who ate the back of our legs. I had time to sort out my pay at the bank (I only had ten rupees left).

Final journey to Manipur Road where we were divided up to be posted to various hospitals in the Arakan. Crossing the Bramaputra was quite an experience – such a huge transit area for Chinese, American, Indian and British. Here we saw the Chinese army taking along their various girlfriends, American troops with Chinese girlfriends and I suppose our boys and the Indians with their companions.

September 20th: 2 am. We arrived at Manipur Road, another huge depot. Matron O'Connor interviewed us and sent us to our wards the next morning. I was thrown in at the deep end by going on night duty. The ward was 'acute medical' with 120 beds, 48 of which were already filled. The floors were mud and the roof was made of banana leaves. My sole companion was a gurkha called Bise Ram – the chowkada or night watchman. I also had three nursing sepoys and was visited by Sister twice nightly.

All the serious diseases were nursed by us. This time we also had mental patients, malnutrition cases and one case of cholera.

During the day we slept in our quarters from 9 until 4, then the bearers brought us tea in our basha (straw hut) bedroom along with water to wash in. The room slept two, mud floor again. Our only furniture was the camp bed, our canvas wash basin and bath plus two thunder boxes in a wee alcove. Here the bearer would peep through a chink in the bamboo lacing to see if we had finished whatever it was we were doing. 'Finished, Miss Sahib? he would ask.

We worked two weeks on night duty, only leaving the ward at midnight for supper in our mess – accompanied always by Bise Ram who led the way with a buttee lantern. Bise Ram and I had a musk rat hunt every night – they are quite large and used to come out to sit and watch us while we sat at the ward desk. We chalked up 18 on the wall in that fortnight.

Back on day duty: No British boys at this stage, but we knew from London we were to nurse IORS. We then had an urgent posting for three of us to go up to 44 IGHC on relief. This was a hospital freshly built at the end of the Ledo Road at Margarita. It is situated on the borders of Burma, India and China. Seven sisters and the Matron were doing everything in a 200-bed hospital centred in a large American base. On our way up by train we stopped at Tinsukeo where we were met by a correspondent of *The Times* who asked us whether we had any food to spare – we managed to produce four hard-boiled eggs.

There was much relief at our arrival. Matron Taplin, who later received the RRC award, was one of the best people I have ever worked for and it was in this hospital that we came up against real nursing – the stuff that Florence Nightingale was made of – and found we were short of so many items. The reason that we came to be so busy was due to a disease known as 'scab typhus' which hit our men. I was allotted two wards of 36 beds each. One ward was full of the typhus cases and the other with so called 'minor illnesses'. We lost seven of our boys in the first week that I was there – it was heartbreaking. The beds kept collapsing because they were made of canvas laid across a wooden frame and due to the humidity the ropes kept breaking.

All we could do for our patients was to wash them down, push fluids where possible and give MOB693 every four hours if we could get it down them. Here the Red Cross came into its own; lemon and glucose, sweets and soap. It was endless work and somehow there was so little hope. It was about ten days before the scab typhus slackened off and the men became convalescent – looking so gaunt and ill.

Christmas Day was one of the worst days for all of us. We lost one of our bravest men, Lance Corporal Fluid, dying to the strains of *Silent Night* played on a wind-up gramophone. I often think that I would have liked to have met his family.

Like the Red Cross today, we took some of our patients out for tea to a local tea planter's bungalow in Ledo. They were so shy. For our relaxation we played mixed hockey twice weekly with a notice being put up on our board in the mess as to who was playing on which side. You know how brilliant the Indians are at playing the game – they played in bare feet. Our other days off became trips into the jungle, lovely picnics and swimming in the mountain rivers.

January 12th 1945: General Hood, the Divisional Medical Officer from Europe, arrived to inspect the hospital. I'm not sure why he came out to us, but he did damn all for our morale so I wrote it in the diary. He made a speech telling us about how wonderful the RAMC (Royal Army Medical Corps) was in Europe and what wonderful supplies they had, then followed this up by telling us that there was no chance of any of us returning home for at least another one and a half years – this to men and Sisters who had already been away from home for two or more years.

The battle continued over the Irawaddy River and we heard that our troops had been cut off, which gave anxious moments to us all. Our wards now had to prepare for the wounded and shell shocked plus a few 'anxiety neuroses' and cocaine druggies. A number had shot off their little finger or toe so that they could be lifted off the battle ground. Most of these men were transferred down the line by train.

One of my two wards was transferred into a surgical ward and I went on night duty again. This time penicillin was being used – a big injection every three hours and I had only nine needles. Forty-eight injections during the night and every patient that you went to you had to lift up the mosquito net and wake him up. My record for one night was 90.

Our men came down from the casualty clearing station which had appalling conditions up at the front so the relief at coming to a bed in a hospital shone in their eyes. Our Matron Taplin and Colonel visited the wards twice a day – even gave us a hand. That must have been one of the finest times of my life; to see such team spirit and support.

At this stage of nursing I came across my first case of gas gangrene in a Gurkha who had had his buttock blown away. I never thought he would survive, but he did. Preparation went on in the wards for the next wave of patients from the front and we continued to make up dressings.

Then on March 1st, 16 coolies came in having been blown up in a lorry which also had cans of petrol in the back (they had come up from Madras and were building the highway into Burma). We had a language problem – Madrasi. They were so badly burned that they looked like mummies lying in bed, and sadly most of them died.

Lady Louis Mountbatten came to see us and spent the afternoon with us before jeeping over to the great US hospital which was more comfortable. I was taken off the wards to host an Indian matron who came to examine the nursing sepoys for upgrading. Also Lady Slim arrived with her companion, Mrs Delph. There was also a wedding for one of the Sisters.

This is about the time that I lost the geese which I was fattening up. You see, all of our live ration came by air in baskets. The Indian expects fresh meat – and got it most of the time. I used to keep some of the ducks and geese back for a week or so in order to fatten them up. One day I looked out from our mess compound to see all of our geese waddling down to the Ledo road with convoys of military vehicles coming in both directions. With some consternation the kitchen sepoys and myself went off to the rescue and all were recovered. With grins on their faces they told me to hold one goose in a pen and then the others would not leave – good advice.

May 3rd: We were on the move. Every item in that hospital had to be packed up. We left only our very ill patients along with biscuit tins to replace the thunder boxes. All the furniture and staff were put on a train of 90 carriages. Matron divided us up into 'quarters' – officers and other ranks. On this journey the geese that I had killed went bad and the ducks nearly got hijacked.

May 8th: War ended in Europe and we heard Churchill's speech on the train.

May 9th: The whole train arrived at Ghauti, a university town in Assam and very civilised. The hospital packing up was off to Rangoon.

May 14th: Victory Day in Ghauti. A number of us marched in a parade on the football ground. The salute was proudly taken by Generals Rankin and Jaunce of the USA. There were fireworks later. We then left for a month in Calcutta.

August 15th: Victory over the Japs at last – organised a VEJ dance before going on night duty again. I was then posted to 93 IGHC but with no information as to where it was. However, on arrival in Calcutta we were told that the unit had already sailed and that we were to follow on. In the meantime we went to Ranchi where the big hospital was nursing and rehabilitating our POWs. We then received orders to move within 24 hours. Matron invited me to take charge of the draft and all its luggage.

Another week in the Calcutta transit camp and then we were off to Singapore in the *Largs Bay*, calling in at Madras to pick up more troops. We arrived on December 1st.

The following six months were not my happiest. The war in Japan was over and instead of nursing as we had done in Assam, our wards were filled with skin diseases and VD. The hospital was in the grounds of St Joseph's Convent on the Changi Road. The buildings were reasonable but every screw and metal object had been lifted so we had no doors or windows. This made us very vulnerable since we were also on the sea front. Some of the VD patients were chained to the walls.

I was asked to help in the mess again and was grateful. Food was in short supply and uninteresting. We were really on iron rations and I learned how to cook corned beef in many ways. The whole atmosphere had changed – especially with the attitude between the nursing sister from Europe (who had joined us) and the VADs.

At last June 1946 arrived and we were on our way home on the *Britannia* to Liverpool. This was my home port and it was lovely to disembark with all of my family waiting for me – it was nearly two years since I had last seen them.

⤷◦⬦◦⬷

Hospital welfare in France

Betty Fuller, Puriton

I had a very busy and sometimes exciting war for four years as organiser of the youth department of the Cambridge branch of the Red Cross – which covered Cambridgeshire and the Isle of Ely. So I was out most evenings driving round the country in the blackout, alone, training youth groups in First Aid, which I loved. However, when D-Day came I knew I had to get nearer to the action. At that time the Red Cross was appealing for volunteers for Hospital Welfare with the Second Army, so I volunteered.

We had about three weeks' training in London and then I and another girl found ourselves aboard an LST (Landing Ship, Tank) bound for Normandy with 102 British General Hospital. We had a tough crossing and the sisters who had had a farewell party the night before were all laid out, but Thelma and I were fine and crossed on the bridge so had a good view of what was coming. We landed on the beach at Courseilles and were welcomed by a company of Pioneers from Suffolk who embraced us – we were the first women they had seen for some time – and gave us awful ration tea made with condensed milk and sugar!

We then set up hospital in large tents under the apple trees in orchards outside Bayeux. Our job was to distribute comforts – most men came in without even a toothbrush – and to talk to the patients and write letters for them. I developed a routine of taking down shorthand all morning and typing and despatching in the afternoon. The weather was lovely then, but steadily the action moved further away and the hospital emptied as the patients went back to the UK and we began to wonder what would happen to us, when we were suddenly collected by truck and whisked off to

Brussels for re-posting. I was sent to a casualty clearing station at Hasselt and there we were busier than ever – most men wanted messages sent home. We were there for the Rhine crossing and the Ardennes breakthrough – both too near for comfort and we were told we should be taken prisoner, not evacuated. However, all was well and again the action moved away.

I was then posted back to Brussels to meet POWs on their way home as more and more camps were liberated – I was out at the airfield all the evening of VE Day so did not get caught up in all the jollification. But within a week or so the war was over and I was sent to Hamburg to liaise with all the hospitals in north Germany including Berlin, now in Russian hands, but the war was behind us and that is another story.

We were in the thick of the doodle bugs
Biddy Matthews, Barrington

In 1940 one of our farming friends offered me a job as a

Biddy Matthews.

milkmaid, and said I could look after his hunters. I did not feel that was right, I had to join up at 18, so I chose the WRNS. I was seventeen and a half and had to have parental permission, so Dad said, 'No, you know what sailors are' (so later on I married one).

In the meantime, having fallen in love as one does at 18, I met a young officer who said I would look nice in a nurse's uniform. Nowadays that would be an unusual observation, but I decided I would volunteer for that anyway. My interview with Matron was a harrowing experience, because I had no qualifications, academically. I was too young to take the High Grades, and shorthand and typing were not of much use. She asked me what my hobbies were and when I said I loved horses, she told me, 'If you can look after animals you can care for people', so I was in.

There were 18 of us initially in our pupil training school. Our tutor was the instigator of 14 days' pre-nursing experience, the first ever, so we settled down into the routine. I made life-long friends, and we worked together, with great realisation that this was our life's work and enjoyed it so much. At the end of the first year four had left, and there were only eight who finished their training.

We were in the thick of the doodlebugs, with aircraft battles overhead, soldiers everywhere, and the days spent working long hours, but on our off duty we had dancing and the few cinemas left in town. Never a shortage of escorts, of course.

Every year we had three months away working at an Auxiliary Hospital. This was at Black Notley some way from home, living in Nissen huts, and very busy indeed. We were getting wounded soldiers and experiencing at 19 the full realisation of what the war meant. We were near to Great Saling which was suddenly in the news. Vast numbers of Americans seemed to be in evidence, and the whole place changed. There was a US Army hospital up the road, there were huge huts there, always aircraft flying overhead, and of course the bliss of being invited to their dances. The food and the romanticism of them was overwhelming. They were so well behaved towards women, and really were very polite and gentle, the ones I met anyway. The time passed too quickly, then it was back to Southend General to nurse in the hospital. By then people were returning to the town, the wards were opened that had been closed and we were all very busy.

Exams and study combined to add to our general exhaustion after the long days on the wards. We still had lectures, usually when we had done twelve hours on night duty, and it was difficult to get through the routine of the day. I could go home when I had my three hours off on day duty, and sometimes I managed to go for a day and a night without sleep, if there were any old friends appearing or dancing dates.

In May 1944 we had dances in the dining room of our hospital, and I met my future husband at one. We used to invite sailors from HMS *Westcliff*, and he was stationed there, but his home was only six miles from where my parents lived.

Shortly afterwards Matron told us to pack a small bag, don't ring up your family, as we are expecting you to have to go away shortly on duty. There was a lot of activity in the town, ships were in the estuary, we were getting different nationalities as patients into the wards.

On 23rd May we were told to be ready to leave. No indication was given of our destination, except that we were to nurse the second front casualties. I wrote letters, and managed to get home for half an hour to collect extra clothes.

On Saturday, 26th May about 20 of us were taken to an EMS hospital at Orsett. These were emergency hospitals set up during the war, to accommodate casualties, and at Black Notley the hospital there was under the same category. We were sleeping in the attic of a very old building, very draughty and on the floor we had straw mattresses so it wasn't at all comfortable, but we were too excited to mind very much. Beds arrived later which made sleeping an improvement. After settling in we went to the wards. There were endless comings and goings of army vehicles, and although not really acceptable the wards had been prepared as best as could be expected. After the preparations had been made it was a question of waiting. We were allowed to go on leave, if we could return in a hurry, but had to be back by the Tuesday evening. We heard the drumming of aeroplane engines all through the night and were unable to sleep. Later we could hear the sound from the docks of ships' sirens and general clatter. The invasion had started and we were told to be prepared. We had had several quite severely injured patients, through accidents, in the ward, but it was cleared for action. On Thursday, the 9th I had written in my diary: 'patients being admitted, terrible sights, all nationalities, all kinds of men, in different states of injury and sickness'. It was my job to 'special' the dying and extremely ill boys. They were unable to write to their parents, so we tried our best to write short notes to tell their relatives they were safe in England.

Fortunately in one way, there were fewer patients than were expected. The worst of the casualties had been landed on the south coast, Littlehampton and the Sussex ports; we had the remainder where they were sorted out into state of injury, and some were sent to specialist units for their treatment, particularly for head or abdomenal wounds. The less seriously injured could be posted nearer home. We were left with the ones that couldn't be moved at once. I remember a handsome young parachute soldier sitting bolt upright in his bed for most of the day. His back had been fractured, but no word of complaint.

We had a contingent of VAD, Red Cross nurses; these I had worked with before at Black Notley and found them most able, some taking up the profession and doing well. They were left to inject the injured with anti-tetanus serum, and this was done to all the patients. Unfortunately the Americans and other nationalities had had a standing long-lasting injection, so they became very ill, because of the excess serum they were given. We had all nationalities, some were Germans. Dutch, French, anyone who had taken part in the invasion. The Desert Rats, who had done their stint in North Africa, were there. We had cases of gas gangrene due to the wounds getting infected. There were amputations, but the bravery and joking even in this condition made us very proud of them all. No word of complaint. The worst part was when we had the parents visiting the dying, quite a few from Scotland, heart breaking, because there was nothing we could really say to them.

Amazingly the intakes had ceased. Time began to be spared for a little fun and games. I was locked into the padded cell by some boisterous young men, the sight of the strait jacket was enough to frighten anyone, and made me pleased to think it was just a relic and not in use any more.

After ten days we were being moved back to Southend Hospital as the wards there were in need of our services. This interlude in my life, which I will never forget, is the subject of this story. I fervently hope that this experience will never be repeated again.

There was always toast

Doris Jones, Bickenhall

At the age of 18 all women had a call to do work of national importance. There were a few choices – the forces, land army, munitions factory or hospitals. I chose hospitals and started work as a ward maid. The main hospital was a beautiful old building, a lovely cottage hospital, with a fine entrance hall, but I was working in 'the huts', which were built for the wounded men. They were long huts with about 30 beds in each one.

I started as a ward maid, but later I was sent to work in a hut where sisters and nurses came for their meals: breakfast 7.30 am to 9 am; lunch 1 pm to 2 pm; tea 4 pm to 5 pm; and supper 7.30 pm to 9 pm. I worked all sorts of hours; three people doing different shifts. Nurses from all over the British Isles were sent to the hospital, lots leaving home for the first time. I was lucky living near the hospital, but I felt sorry for many of the young nurses, but I was able to help with a few things (like saving eggs which were to be boiled for them to have with bacon and sausage later on in the week). There was always toast, but 2 oz butter, put out on a Sunday, didn't last long. I worked there for five or six years.

Two nights of 'blitz'

Bunty Meager, Barwick and Stoford

In 1938 I was 17 years old and sent to the Norland Institute in London, to train as a nursery nurse. I was a 'maiden' and as such had to answer the door, wait at table etc. When a 'door maiden', I answered the door to a lady and showed her to the waiting room. I then asked her name and she answered, 'Will you be long?' so that is what I wrote on the card to take to the Principal, Miss Whitehead. Miss Whitehead was not amused!

Another episode I remember well was when another maiden upset a tureen of lentil soup all over herself! Luckily it was not hot. We had a laugh taking her to the bathroom for a wash down!

No showers in those days. Also waiting at table was a hazard, soup in laps, baked potatoes under the table instead of on top.

In 1939 we were evacuated to Berkshire. Then we were evacuated again to Hothfield Place, a large mansion in Kent, with suits of armour in the hall etc. One thing I remember about being here was the arrangement of the children's toilets at the top of some stairs. There were eight seats arranged in a semi-circle on which children were perched whilst the little ones sat on potties arranged on the stairs leading up. What a sight!

The basement at Hothfield had had two children's baths installed as there was only one other bathroom in the whole house. After the children were in bed we nurses used to sit two to a bath for our evening wash! One evening we had a visitor: the butler to Lord Hothfield. With half a dozen nude women sitting two to a bath in the basement, he soon made a hasty retreat!

We had a lovely winter at Hothfield as it snowed quite heavily. We had the 'Bethnal Greenies' with us and took it in turns to look after a lovely bunch of children aged from two to five years from Bethnal Green. From there we were once again evacuated, this time to Devon where I took my final exams to be a Norland Nurse.

After qualifying in 1941, I acquired a post with Mr and Mrs Tait at Wotton House, Eton College, Windsor. I was in charge of three children, two boys aged seven and five and a girl of two. I did not enjoy being in a big household with a butler and other staff. I was neither one of the staff nor one of the family, but I did enjoy being sent off to Cornwall with Mrs Tait and the children. We stayed in a bungalow at Trethevy which was great. We spent most of the summer on the beach. We had to collect mussels off the rocks and bracken from the cliff tops to eat. We had a local lady in to clean and she liked her Cornish pasty 'dipped in tay' (tea)! I used to walk up through the woods to a farm occupied by our milkman and his family. I often had Cornish pasties with them. They were Mr and Mrs Collett. They had a young son, Holman.

When we returned to Eton I decided to give in my notice and take up some part time employment until I could start my training as a children's nurse at the BCH – Bristol Children's Hospital.

I commenced my training at the BCH in 1942. I thoroughly enjoyed it and made great friends with Mary Reynolds, known as Rennie. We lived in the nurses' home but frequently went home to my aunt in Bristol who had looked after me from the age of five until I was twelve.

All nursing staff at the BCH had to do a month or more at the emergency hospital at Weston Super Mare. While there we had a rude awakening as to what war was about – we had two nights of 'blitz'. The sirens went and we had to wear our hard hats and rescue all the children from the wards and take them to the basement. As it happened some of the children had chicken pox … or was it measles? … and I'm sorry to say they got mixed up with some of the children who hadn't had whichever disease it was! However, all the children came through the experience safe and unhurt.

The day after the bombing I took a walk to visit two aunts who lived nearby and who ran a small school. They were well and unaffected by the blitz. However, I walked into their garden and picked up an incendiary bomb (quite mad) … and took it back to the hospital where it was defused!

We had quite a bit of fun with the RAF boys stationed there and my friend Rennie eventually married one of them.

On returning to the BCH we were on night duty and got to know the 'fire watchers' who were on the top floor of the hospital, which had been closed for the duration of the war. The fire watch used to come down at night and help us catch cockroaches in the ward kitchens. I took my final exams in April 1945 and passed to become an RSCN: Registered Sick Children's Nurse.

The BCH was situated at the top of St Michael's Hill. There were six large wards and other rooms. The children were aged from nought to 16 years and all kinds of problems were admitted. The two wards at the top of the building, as I mentioned, were closed during the war. Of the remaining four, one was a ward for babies. Some had bad eczema and their arms had to be splinted to stop them scratching themselves, poor little things. They were also covered in different lotions, i.e. gentian violet and tar ointments. Most of the babies were bottle fed but some mothers came in to feed their babies.

Other wards were for general surgery – one small boy about a year old had to have one leg amputated due to cancer. I sometimes wonder how he progressed; adapted quite well I expect. There were large balconies where TB patients had to sleep outside for the fresh air!

Another ward was for tonsils and adenoids. That was not a nice ward to be on when the children came round from anaesthetic! In those days children were not allowed visitors! Not even Mum and Dad. They had to peer through a small window in the door. I think, looking back, that this was a very unkind rule as the little ones must have thought their parents had deserted them. We also had to work in theatre which was very interesting.

After completing my training at the BCH I worked in the Chesterfield Nursing Home in Clifton. While there Armistice was declared and we nurses went to join the crowd in the Bristol Centre to cheer and enjoy the fact the war had ended. We were late getting back to the nurses' home and had to climb in through the window. Nurses had to be in by 10 pm in those days.

We wore a pink uniform and little caps
Peggy Williams, Curry Rivel

When the war started in 1939 the Americans wanted to help England in some way, and one thing they did was to form an Anglo American War Relief Fund. Some of the money was given so that the children of London could get into the country. Thus five big houses were taken over to turn into nurseries: Dyrham Park (now National Trust), Bath; Marsh Court, Bristol; Dauntsey Park, Chippenham; Chapel Cleeve, Minehead; and Tapley Park, Instow in Devon. I trained to be a nursery nurse from 1943 to 1945, and I began at Dauntsey Park, for two years. Later I went to Dyrham Park and Chapel Cleeve.

We had about 60 children from two months to five years, from Stepney and Bermondsey, a matron, a sister, a nursery school teacher, five staff nurses and about 20 students. Each house was divided into four nurseries. We wore a pink uniform and little

Evacuees being cared for at an Anglo-American nursery in Wiltshire.

caps, and worked eight-hour shifts from 6 am to 8 pm with night duty from 8 pm to 6 am, which we did for a month every so often. We had a little time off each day, with a day off weekly and a weekend four times a year.

A typical day's routine was: waking children at 7 am, dressing and giving breakfast in own nursery, 'potting' the little ones, the others to the loo, before going for a walk, playing indoors or outside. Can you imagine dressing up 20 two to three year olds in coats, hats and scarves and gloves on a cold winter's day? In for lunch and then an hour's 'rest' on their beds, then up for games or walks before 'high tea' about 5 pm. At 6 pm we started getting them to bed (baths were on a rota) and lastly settled by 8 pm by the night staff. We had to clear up the nursery and put the clothes out for the next day. The children had their own clothes, plus lots more sent over from America.

The night duty started at 8 pm – visiting all four nurseries, then settling down to mending, darning and ironing. 'Potting' was done about 11 pm before settling down, but keeping an ear open for children needing attention. Before our duty finished at 6 am we prepared breakfast trays for the children and staff. The three and a half to five year olds had a nursery school teacher who gave educational games, reading etc to the children in the mornings.

Staff were allowed to take a child out for the day if desired, to nearby villages. Parents could visit occasionally, but few did as it was too expensive to travel from London, most sent cards and letters. At five years old the child had to return to London – others would replace them.

As enemy action decreased so the children were taken home, leaving less children in the nurseries, so they were gradually shut down – Dauntsey first, so I went to Dyrham Park, then Chapel Cleeve until VE Day. All the time we were studying for our Nursery Nurses Examination – theory and practical – I think most of us passed. It was a very happy time for me and led me on to my career.

CHAPTER 5

Teaching

Through air raids and evacuation, teachers continued to care for their young charges, some even accompanying the children when they left the cities to find safety in the countryside during the blitz. Women teachers were not encouraged to leave their jobs to serve in the forces – as one ex-teacher remembers, unlike the situation for male staff, women were told quite plainly that their job would not be guaranteed for them when they came home again.

We helped to issue gas masks
Hilda Holdsworth, Wedmore

In 1938 I undertook training to be an air raid warden in the event of war breaking out. I learnt how to patrol in the blackout, what to do in an air raid, how to deal with casualties, and how to recognise the different smells of possible poison gases. On completion of the course, and test, supervised by the police force, I was issued with a warrant card and uniform, including a service respirator.

The school closed to pupils while staff attended to the issue of gas masks to the residents of the area. It was pitiful to see the box-like devices issued to parents with small babies. We held meetings of parents to encourage them to enlist their children for evacuation in the event of the outbreak of war. Some recalcitrant parents objected to losing their child benefit, as of course the money would be paid to the householders in the reception area.

Evacuation took place in September 1939 – two days before the outbreak of war, and even staff did not know where they were going, but when we began to recognise passing stations we were able to make guesses. We arrived at Todmorden on the Lancashire-Yorkshire border and billeting officers took over, as householders took on their new responsibilities. Only two staff stayed behind because of the numbers – myself and the woodworking master. We were billeted on a woman member of the staff, much older than we were. No bathroom, so bath nights were events – hip bath on the kitchen floor with hot water from the set pot boiler!

Some children were so homesick that their parents took them back to Bradford by half term. There had been no air raids at all.

Many children were evacuated to escape the bombing and continued their education in the safety of the countryside.

We had an outbreak of German measles which worried the hostesses – responsibility for other people's children is never easy.

After Christmas the woodwork teacher was back in Bradford and I stayed on until Easter, by which time very few of our children remained. On my return I found the school much changed because it was partly equipped to operate as a Reception Centre for bombed out people.

I then left Bradford to work in a Secondary Boys School in Hounslow, where I did four years in Lee Boys School.

Men in teaching were due for call-up to the age of 35 unless they had already got their headship. Servicemen were guaranteed their own jobs back after demob, but women teachers were told if they enlisted in the WRAC, WRNS or WAAF their jobs were not assured after the war.

We were hardy in those days
Molly Wilson, The Charltons

I remember standing beside my doctor mother at a country railway station checking evacuee children for obvious health problems.

I was a teacher at that time, first in Stamford and later Keswick. If the air raid warning went during the night at Stamford we had to get up and settle the 30 or so boarders to sleep on the cloakroom floor before joining them. The only real trouble while I was there was a bomb that buried itself in the substantial wall of someone's kitchen without exploding, so part of the town had to be evacuated until it was made safe; and one murky November afternoon the warning went so the children were sent home early, and a German plane dived over the station machine-gunning it. The girls flung themselves flat and no one was hurt. They rather enjoyed it in fact, though I expect the bullet marks on the building can still be seen.

At Keswick, Derwentwater froze. That only happens after ten days of continuous frost with no snow to spoil the surface for skating. The headmaster cancelled afternoon school so the children could all go skating as he said it was the chance of a lifetime. I think the last time it happened was in 1897. I used to teach in a wooden hut heated by a coke stove, and had to keep a temperature chart. It was usually around 48F, which was all right as we were dressed for it. I wore three layers of wool topped by a leather jacket, with either furry boots or ankle socks. One day we were so hot that I opened all the windows and the door. It was 60F. On the other hand when I opened up one day the aquarium was frozen almost solid and the poor little fish was swimming around in the middle of a block of ice. That, I decided, was really too cold, so the children ran about outside until the room had warmed up a bit – to about 40F. We were hardy in those days.

In July 1944 London was under attack from the V1s and a party of mothers with very young children were evacuated to Keswick. The headmaster opened up the junior school to them by ending term early for our children, and I found myself running a nursery school for toddlers, which was rather different from what I was used to.

By that time I had realised that the war was coming to an end and had volunteered to join the Friends' Ambulance Unit, as I wanted to do relief work. That meant six months' hospital training, so in September I joined a section in an emergency hospital at Burntwood near Lichfield and was put to work in a ward of men with fractured femurs and other wounds. I well remember being woken early one morning as there was a convoy coming in and everyone was needed. They were the wounded from Arnhem. I was giving out breakfasts when I saw one man sitting bolt upright in bed with a commando knife stuck in the top of his locker. When I commented he said, 'You can have it if you like, but don't cut cake with it. I used it to kill Germans.' He was a Pole who spoke perfect English, and later taught me a few words of Polish so that I could communicate with the two other Poles in the ward after he left. The most useful was the word for good. You can go a long way with that using different inflections.

After three months there I was sent to St Mary's Islington to the maternity ward to learn how to deliver a baby should the need arise when we were in the field (not a green field, you understand, but the field of work!). I did actually help to deliver one baby, but when I was in the field, fortunately, there were no expectant mothers.

While I was at St Mary's the V2s were occasionally falling. I'd been frightened of bombs, but the V2s exploded before you heard them coming, so no anticipation and therefore no fright. The V1s were different as I found out when one inexplicably came over – inexplicable because the launching pads were by then in Allied hands. I was making a bed with another nurse when we heard the unmistakable sound, and it was as though we were in a film with the camera running slowly. The mothers slowly took their pillows and put them over the cots to protect the babies from flying glass. The nurse's face whitened – she had been in a hospital that had been hit – and we stopped moving. The sound grew louder and thankfully fainter and the little London sparrow of a Mum said, 'That's okay then', and took back her pillow, and everything went back to normal speed and I realised for the first time exactly what it had been like living in London the previous year.

Then in April we went for further training, still in London, and one day were summoned to a meeting in an empty ward in the Middlesex Hospital to be told that we would be part of the first convoy of relief workers to go into Germany.

CHAPTER 6

Transport

Keeping Britain moving was essential as the very fabric of society seemed to be crumbling beneath the blitz. People still had to get to work, and military traffic had to move about the country, crowding the trains as well as the roads. For young women, employment could be as varied as single-handedly running a busy signalbox on an inter-city rail route (at the age of 18) or coping with the difficulties of taking fares in the blackout as a 'clippie' – the affectionate name for the female bus conductors. The civil airline routes, too, had to be kept open and BOAC operated throughout the war years. Their work involved women in great military events – even the simple task of producing pilots' handbooks for the Air Ministry could be memorable when the pilots in question were the Dambusters of 617 Squadron!

I was an LNER Signalwoman
Molly Kelly, Bickenhall and District

For my war work I chose to work as a signalwoman on the London & North Eastern Railway (LNER). I started work in 1941 and left in 1947 when I got married. My first job was at Wormald Green cabin near Ripon under the direction of Mr Bob Selby, with whom I kept in touch until 2003, when he died at the age of 91.

Manning the signal box at Littlethorpe.

I went to York Railway Museum to study two days a week, where I was taught to do Morse Code to enable me to signal trains, which all worked on different codes. At the age of 18 I was put in charge of Littlethorpe cabin near Harrogate. I lived in a farmhouse near to the cabin but the lodgings were not very good. Littlethorpe cabin was on the main line from Kings Cross to Edinburgh and I had a level crossing and sidings to look after which meant me pulling levers to change the points. When it was foggy I had to put detonators on the lines to warn the train drivers to slow down. I worked three shifts – 6 am to 2 pm, 2 pm to 10 pm and 10 pm to 6 am, and every three weeks I finished at 1 pm on Saturday until 10 pm on Monday.

I was in direct contact with York Control at all times and had a coal fire plus an oven in the cabin. The firemen used to drop coal off for me but I received that much that the Station Master stopped them. The local policeman used to come for a cup of tea when I was on nights and one night a prisoner who had escaped from the prisoner of war camp nearby came and sat on the cabin steps. He made no attempt to talk to me or get in the cabin, he was just trying to get on a goods train to get away. The policeman was never there when you needed him but I didn't feel threatened. I really enjoyed my war work.

I was a bus conductress

Jean Holland, Wiveliscombe

I joined London Transport as a 'clippie' a few weeks after I married in June 1944. The first two weeks were spent in school at Chiswick, and working on buses under the guidance of an experienced conductor. It was quite something mixing with and meeting so many people, and also travelling on so many different bus routes throughout London.

Although we did not have the heavy bombing at that time, we did have the 'buzz bombs', as we called the V1 rockets. Several times when we were en route we would hear the engines on them stop and immediately the bomb would drop, causing major damage, sometimes perilously close to where we were.

My first day out on my own was daunting; I was given a driver who seemed very ancient to me at this time. He kept starting off from the bus stop before I could ring the bell to tell him it was safe to do so. However, I soon learnt to cope with the different temperaments of the drivers; most seemed very much older than me, because all the younger men were in the forces. We did shift work and on the early shift the first bus left the depot at Upton Park at 4.30 am. I lived about 35 minutes from the depot, which meant catching the first train out in the morning. This was a steam train and it left my station at 3.45 am. On the late shifts we finished around half past midnight. I was usually able to get the last train but on one occasion had to walk arriving home at 4 o'clock in the morning. It was very difficult operating the bus in the blackout, having to recognise where you were with no lights, taking fares and giving change in the dark with only the use of a mini torch attached to your lapel. This was on buses that were brim-full with passengers too, with sometimes as many as ten standing in the aisle on the upper deck as well as the lower one. It was an absolute godsend when we had a lovely moonlit night to work in.

I was given a regular driver after about six weeks. He had red hair and a red moustache. His name was Bill (Tug) Wilson and he was probably around 50 but thought he was a teenager. He was a proper torment. He would tap on the window for me to come

Female clippies became a common sight during the war years.

round to the front of the bus, then he would drive off so I was left running along behind it. On one occasion he tipped all my box of tickets out in the middle of Green Street, Upton Park. This was a very busy road and I had to collect all the tickets up again. It was a good job for him that I was able to laugh at his antics. One day when working we experienced a very loud explosion close enough to shake the bus a little. We all thought it was a bomb although we had heard nothing and no air raid siren had sounded. We were told later that it was a gas explosion, only to discover the real truth – it was one of the first V2 rockets to fall on the outskirts of London. It had been a direct hit on a house in Dagenham.

Being a clippie was lovely and even now 60 years on I still say it was my favourite job. I laughed almost all day at the antics of people and met the very best of our London folk, and being able to help the forces from other countries find their way around London was just great. VE Day has special memories for me. I was on a route around Trafalgar Square that evening. Traffic had been brought to a halt by the massed crowds. There was such joy everywhere, people were laughing, singing, crying and dancing. It was really wonderful. When I see the old newsreels on the television I can pick out our bus because we had American sailors on the very top of it. All the American servicemen coming down the stairs to get off were giving me money, most of them gave a £1 note each time for drinks for me and the driver to celebrate. This indeed was a lot of money. Even now I still think of the time I spent with London Transport with great fondness, and I'm sure I will never forget it.

I was in the Merchant Air Service
Marian Reddington, Burnham-on-Sea

After education at Redland High School for Girls in Bristol, followed by a course at Bristol College of Domestic Subjects and further training by J. Lyons and Co, at their school for executive and managerial staff, I spent my whole working life in the catering industry, before and after the outbreak of the Second World War.

My mother was taken seriously ill in 1942 and I went back to Bristol to assist her. After she recovered, I returned to catering and obtained a position with the national airline, British Overseas Airways Corporation (BOAC).

Marian Reddington.

I was firstly employed as under-manageress of catering at the Corporation's ancillary engineering establishment in Brislington, Bristol. Within a few months I was approached by a senior member of the catering staff and taken to the RAF station at Lyneham in Wiltshire, where it was intended that BOAC would set up a base for Dakota and Liberator transport aircraft to operate to the Middle East and countries in neutral Europe, to supplement the services already in operation from Bristol's airport at Whitchurch.

I was supplied with an assortment of second-hand equipment and other artefacts and instructed to set up a catering unit in the partitioned-off part of an aircraft hangar. The aim was to provide refreshments and meals to working ground engineers, administration staff, flying crews, the expected passengers that would pass through and to provision aircraft as required. I accepted the challenge, found myself accommodation in the locality, proceeded to recruit suitable staff and solicited local suppliers. After initial teething troubles, the operation got under way and the flying services duly commenced and increased as time went by.

During my service at Lyneham my status changed and I became 'uniform staff' with the designation of Catering Officer. The uniform comprised a navy-blue, double-breasted tunic with brass buttons, with the rank marking of one gold ring, surmounted by a pink one (to indicate 'catering'), navy-blue skirt, white shirt, black tie, stockings and flat shoes, plus a navy-blue 'fore and aft' cap with pink piping and a gold-coloured badge.

The regular services operated from Lyneham were to Cairo via Algiers and along the North African coast, with 'special' services to other destinations, including Tehran and Moscow.

The only passengers who flew on Corporation aircraft at this time were persons important to the war effort, including diplomatic staff, service personnel, politicians, war correspondents, members of ENSA (the forces' entertainment service) and similar. I encountered many well known personalities, including, amongst others, the Russian Ambassadors, Mr Maisky and his successor Mr Molotov, Mrs Winston Churchill, Mr Churchill's physician Lord Moran, the Viceroy of India's wife and daughter, Lady Wavell, General de Gaulle and his daughter; of the entertainers who passed through I remember Gracie Fields and George Formby.

After D-Day in June 1944 and as Europe was gradually liberated, destinations were opened up to civil aviation again and the RAF relinquished their control over the main London pre-war air terminal at Croydon and non-military operations recommenced. In August 1944 I was transferred from Lyneham to Croydon to assist with the busy traffic passing through. One day in September I was awaiting the arrival of 14 foreign Air Attaches when I noticed a rather dishevelled soldier, in combat kit, at the reception hall entrance, I approached and asked if I could help him and would he care for a cup of tea? (I guessed he had just returned from Arnhem.) He replied, 'A cuppa Rosie Lea! Not 'alf, I haven't had a decent cuppa for weeks'. He then put two fingers in his mouth and let forth a shrill whistle and shouted to his companions outside, 'Come on, mates. There's a cuppa Rosie Lea.' During the next few days a number of British and American aircraft brought in survivors of Operation Market Garden. This was a highlight of my BOAC service and I felt honoured to serve these men.

Shortly after, I was posted again, this time to RAF Leuchars in Fife, where BOAC were operating flights over occupied Norway, to Sweden, Finland and with occasional services to Leningrad and Moscow. The main object of these services, apart from maintaining diplomatic connections, was to transport the highly specialised ball bearings manufactured in Sweden by Skefko for use in aircraft production and other industries in the UK. Also a large amount of prisoner-of-war and other mail was airlifted. Many important persons passed through on missions to Scandinavia and Russia, including Lord Lovat, Admiral Lord Frazer, Sir Walter Elliott, Stephen King-Hall, as well as escaped prisoners-of-war and displaced persons. Whilst at Leuchars, I met my future husband who was a Radio Officer flying on these routes.

When the European war finally ended the BOAC station at Leuchars was closed down and the operations moved to Croydon. I was transferred to the old Bristol Airport at Whitchurch, where I was in charge of catering at the arrival/departure side of the airfield and the Flying Training School.

It is not generally known, or appreciated, that the Merchant Air Service, like the Merchant Navy, operated during the war to Empire and neutral destinations, in completely unarmed and unescorted defenceless aircraft, and assisted greatly in the air transportation of service personnel and equipment throughout the war zones. A large number of RAF men were flown to the Continent at the outbreak of hostilities and were subsequently evacuated after France collapsed. Flying boats from Cairo were used to evacuate troops from Crete and land planes from Cairo carried personnel and equipment and evacuated wounded during the North African campaign. The return ferry service (flying pilots and crews back to the USA and Canada after they had delivered warplanes to the UK) was also operated by BOAC from 1941 onwards. This operation undoubtedly helped to lay the foundation for the post-war transatlantic routes. The airline was also involved in supplying foodstuffs and equipment to the beleaguered island of Malta during the long siege, the aircraft operating overnight to and from the island, at great risk, from Gibraltar.

A considerable number of aircraft were lost due to enemy action and accidents caused through the operational difficulties experienced and many air crews and ground staff lost their lives in service.

I was a draughtswoman in the Air Ministry
Mary Goulstone, Combe Florey

During the 1939–1945 war I was in firstly the Ministry of Aircraft Production and then the Air Ministry, employed as a temporary draughtswoman to replace a member of the staff who had been called up.

We were responsible for the publication of technical handbooks for pilots. One of the books we produced was for the Lancaster bombers used during the Dambusters Raid in 1943, which was one of the important projects which helped to diminish the strength of the German war effort.

The 'Bouncing Bombs' as they were called, were designed by Barnes Wallis, who was on the staff of Messrs Vickers Aviation. He was the brilliant inventor and designer of the R100 airship, which crossed the Atlantic in the 1920s. He also designed the well-known Wellington aircraft and the huge Tallboy bombs which destroyed the *Tirpitz* and much else, but he only became better known following the invention of the 'Bouncing Bombs', designed to bounce across water. They were dropped over reservoirs in the Ruhr valley in Germany, including those of the Mohne and Eder Dams, where they successfully detonated against the dam walls which then gave way and disrupted the working capacity of the Ruhr industrial district.

The bombs were in the shape of, for want of a better description, a Heinz baked bean tin and because they had to be carried by the Lancaster bombers in a horizontal position, the

TRANSPORT

bomb-carrying mechanism had to be adapted. So we were involved in considerable Top Secret work to get the pilots' handbooks out in time for the raid, which was scheduled to coincide with the night when moonlight would assist in locating the targets.

As the world was told after the raid, it was successful, although some of the Lancasters of 617 Squadron did not return home. Another great sadness was that we learned a few days after the raid that the Germans had housed a number of prisoners of war just below the dams and they all lost their lives.

Barnes Wallis was awarded the CBE and later knighted for his work. On his death in 1979, a memorial service was held in St Paul's Cathedral, which I was invited to attend, together with many others who had helped in the work. The Prince of Wales read the lesson and the address was given by Dr Morpurgo. As we all filed out of the Cathedral after the service, the organist played the *Dambusters March*.

CHAPTER 7

Communications

The 'Hello' girls were responsible for keeping communications open, even when air raids flattened the streets and factories around them. In those days of manual telephone exchanges, operators responded personally to each caller and although they might have been merely 'a small cog in a very big wheel', they were of the greatest importance, whether as a civilian manning a factory switchboard at night, in case of air raids, after working all day, or in uniform with the Royal Corps of Signals.

I was a 'Hello' girl

Olive Lane, Puriton

I was 15 when the Second World War was declared and working as an office junior in London. When I was 16 I obtained work with the London Telecommunications Region (LTR) East Area. The LTR had lost so many of its staff to the forces during the early months of the war that a Reserved Occupation ruling was brought in. This applied to young and old members of staff alike, and of course it included me although to begin with I was too young to be conscripted, but it meant I was there for the duration.

After seven weeks' training I passed the entrance test with flying colours and then two days after this in September 1940 the bombing of London started. On my first day as a fully fledged

A team of 'Hello' girls.

telephonist it took me five hours to get to East London, a normal journey of one hour. The Chief Supervisor immediately sent me home, advising me to report for duty to my nearest exchange the next day. This I did and was there for one week, when I was despatched to a smaller exchange but still not far away from my home.

I liked the work and the 'Hello' girls I worked with and, being the youngest, was hopelessly spoiled. The exchange might have been small but it was an extremely busy one, carrying the lines of several large factories all involved in war work. Our job was to see that communications were kept open which proved extremely difficult from time to time when bombs damaged the cables and lines were down. Sometimes all we had were three working lines to London with all the subscribers clamouring that their call was the most important and would we put their call first. However, all calls were done in strict rotation and being a manual exchange we had to be polite at all times, not always easy when an irate subscriber was on the other end of the line. Apart from all the important calls, we also gave out air raid warnings to some services in our area, ARP posts and other important people who needed to be advised that an air raid was about to start. We dared not make a mistake; people's lives depended on us.

The 'Hello' girls also had to work on a rota with the night staff, as most of the men had been called up, and because of transport difficulties we had to be at the exchange by 6 pm and work until 8 am the next day. Because the hours were so long we worked seven days out of fourteen. Nevertheless, many of the girls liked this duty because they were able to earn extra money and if they were saving up to get married, as many of them were, this helped a great deal so we had no difficulty in changing duties if you did not like the long hours or could not cope with night work.

Our exchange was on the edge of the marshes and on the flight path to London, and we were also close to the big factories and were constantly under the threat of bombing. Some of the bombs were too close for comfort and you could hear them whistling down. The windows all round the switchroom had very heavy metal shutters so we always hoped that we were reasonably safe. The only time I remember them being damaged I was not on duty.

So many people with so many jobs, all of us a small cog in a very big wheel but every one of us working with one another, a community spirit that I will never forget and one I have never seen since. I have now lost many of my colleagues but I still remember them all and I am still in touch with three of them after all these years.

Night duty at the switchboard

Freda Evans, Appley Cross

In 1939 I was living in Altrincham, Cheshire (south of Manchester) and I worked as a secretary in a large engineering factory producing heavy machinery for power stations etc, but as this was a government factory, I was in what was called a reserved occupation, so I was not called up to join the armed forces. However, the factory changed over to aircraft production and of course because of that, was considered to be a legitimate target for German bombers to visit.

To help pull my weight for the war effort I was instructed, one night a week, after I had finished work at 5 pm, to go on switchboard duty all night. The switchboards in those days were a 'hands on' affair with lots of plugs and head-phones, and if there was an air raid I had to raise the alarm if bombs had been dropped on the factory. I would be told where they were and if there were any casualties or fires, and if so I had to call out the firm's fire brigade and ambulance. I always dreaded going on duty as, not being used to operating a switchboard, I thought I might not carry out the correct instructions and so not be at all helpful. However, good fortune was on my side and there were no devastating air raids when I was on duty, so many casualties were probably saved by that fact.

I was in the Royal Corps of Signals
Dorothy House, Puriton

After having been deferred twice (as my boss was a 'big noise' in the local Home Guard and claimed I was helping the war effort by doing his office work) I was called up in October 1942 and sent to Wrexham in North Wales. After the usual period of 'square bashing' I was posted with others of my unit to Queensbury in deepest Yorkshire, to train as a telephonist in the Royal Corps of Signals.

The whole procedure came as a shock! Living in a small village (Puriton) and never having been further afield than Bristol, I felt as though I had been sent abroad! However, time passed as it does of course, and London was the next posting – just for a few weeks until, on my 21st birthday (what a way to spend a birthday), I set off for Salisbury to a hush-hush location, to do my stuff on the switchboard. After a few weeks I had a weekend pass and of course went home to Puriton. On returning to my unit, to my horror I was told I had been posted to somewhere none of my mates had heard of! Imagine my amusement and surprise when I discovered it was to Burnham-on-Sea. So back I travelled to Somerset, to the envy of my fellow workers. My fiancé was a farmer in Puriton so was 'reserved'. As I was back home we decided to get married. Being so near to home, I got lots of 'sleeping out' passes, and of course the inevitable happened. I was discharged in November 1943 'For Family Reasons', as it states on my discharge sheet.

So my war service was a bit of a non-event. However, I treasure my cap badge and my paybook and the 'Good' for military conduct.

CHAPTER 8

Feeding the Nation

On an island immersed in total war, its seas haunted by enemy submarines preventing ships getting through with supplies, good home-produced food was not a luxury but a necessity. As many younger farm labourers joined the armed forces, the Women's Land Army (WLA) called for women to come to work on the land. And come they did, from all walks of life, whether they had grown up in the country or never seen a cow before! In Somerset, just as in every other county, young women could be found ploughing, sowing and harvesting, as well as doing the million and one other farming tasks – and hand-milking dairy herds three times a day. But it was not only the WLA that proved women could keep the country's larders as full as rationing would allow. They were also delivering milk and other necessaries, running provisions shops, poultry farming and much more. Even schoolgirls were exhorted to 'Lend a Hand on the Land' and spent their holidays in the harvest fields or fruit picking.

No regrets in the Land Army

Sylvia Kurjo, Enmore

When I got my call-up papers I chose to join the Women's Land Army (WLA). I knew nothing about working in the countryside, as I was a town girl, working in a big office in London. I think the

Sylvia Kurjo and friends.

first shock was when I received my kit from the postman. There was so much of it! Two pairs of brown trousers like riding breeches, thick warm brown socks up to the knees, dark green long-sleeved V-neck pullover and a very warm three-quarter length brown overcoat, with a matching brown hat which looked something like a cowboy hat! But the things with which I had the most difficulty were the shoes. I was used to tripping around in high heels, so I thought I would never get used to wearing them – black boots and gumboots for work and the strong brown 'sensible' shoes for off duty. Surprisingly enough, they soon became quite comfortable.

So off I went to the railway station to get a train from London to Buckinghamshire, feeling very self-conscious in my new uniform and already a little homesick! I was so pleased to meet up with a couple of other girls feeling the same way. However, we were met off the train and taken to a training centre. There we had lectures, and were taught how to drive a tractor, milk cows, mend fences or hedges, hoe, feed animals, get in the harvest and many other things. After our training we were sent to hostels in different parts of the countryside, or if you wished, you could live on a farm with the farmer and his wife, but that could be rather lonely, so I preferred to live in a hostel with others for company.

It was a hard life; up at 6 o'clock in the morning, a quick breakfast and away in a lorry, being dropped off in a gang to whichever farm needed help that day. The weather could be freezing cold, windy and wet in the winter, and sometimes very hot in the summer. We had to be in by 10 o'clock on a weekday but could have a late pass on a Saturday if we wanted to see a film at the local cinema or go to a dance in the village hall. Most of the girls came from the cities. Before joining up they were office workers, shop assistants, hairdressers and dressmakers, and when it came to country life they were as green as the grass they found there. But, by the spring of 1940 two million new acres of land had been ploughed up, and although during the whole of the war years food was rationed, *bread* was *never* rationed, thanks, some people say, to the Land Army.

Naturally, these girls who didn't know hay from straw at first made mistakes. We used to hear some funny stories. One new girl starting to learn milking, was handed a bucket of soapy water and a cloth by the cowman, and told to get washing. He meant just the cow's udders of course. He went off to do something else and when he came back he found she had carefully washed a cow from head to toe! Another girl was told to harness up a huge carthorse. As she was only about 5 ft tall she had to stand on a box to put the collar on. He lowered his head and she put the collar on, but then he tossed his head up and as she was still holding the collar, up in the air she went with it! So as you can see we had our laughs and happy times as well as our sad times, when some of the girls lost brothers or boyfriends killed in the fighting, or had some bad news from home, but we all supported each other and got on very well considering we were about 40 females eating, sleeping and working together.

The WLA finally closed down in 1950, but 5,000 women wished to stay behind and continue to work on the land. I left in

1947, and quickly settled back into office work after polishing up my typing and shorthand speeds. I often look back on those days though, and have no regrets at all that I chose to join the Women's Land Army.

I was a dairy delivery 'boy'
Margaret Veale, Brompton Regis

I lived in Keynsham, between Bristol and Bath. I went to school in Bristol and left in 1943. I started giving piano lessons, under the supervision of my piano teacher. The following year, as I was 18 years old, I was called up to do war work. There was a vacancy at the local dairy, for a job on their milk round. The hours were 7.15 am to 1.15 pm. This suited me very well as I had the rest of the day free, so was able to carry on teaching piano, as well as study for my LRAM exam.

At first I went out on the round in a van with a Mr Smith, who was too old for the forces, then later on in a horse-drawn milk float with a younger man. Why he wasn't in the forces I don't know, and didn't like to ask. I thoroughly enjoyed that until one day the horse bolted in the High Street amongst all the traffic. The horse was quite spirited and John hadn't much idea how to handle him. When, later on, the horse bolted again I was so shaken I was put back in the van and the boss took over the horse.

It was an interesting job, meeting all sorts of people. We had quite a lot of London evacuees, most of whom were very friendly. Milk was rationed to four pints a week for healthy grown ups, though children and invalids got more, but I can't remember how much. I didn't worry about the weather as I have always enjoyed the outdoor life.

One outstanding pleasure I used to look forward to was going to the bakery – a few doors away – mid-morning and buying a hot chelsea bun, straight from the oven, to have with my mid-morning drink with my friend Mary, whom I first met when she came to work at the dairy. Mary married a local boy, so did I and we have all been friends ever since.

We milked out of doors all the year round
Thelma Harding, Coxley & District

At the end of June 1943 I was 19 and a typist in a London office. Not wishing to be called up to work in a factory, as two of my colleagues had been, I decided to volunteer for the Women's Land Army. Having done so, I was asked to go for an interview. 'What would you like to do?' I was asked: the timber corps, tractor driving, fieldwork or I could be a rat catcher! I decided I would quite like to do dairy work.

So at the end of August 1943 I was sent to Steanbow Farm at Pilton for four weeks' training. This was a farm that had been taken over by the War Agricultural Executive Committee (commonly known as the War Ag) for the training of land girls. At the end of the first two weeks we all became aware of muscles we never knew we had, but we all had a laugh about ourselves and enjoyed each other's company.

Many girls were sent to Steanbow Farm for training.

At the end of the four-week training I was sent to work on a farm near Axbridge – this was not a happy experience on the whole. Unfortunately not all the girls ended up at nice places. However, I contacted the local Land Army representative and she was quite happy to find me another farm to go to. This was in Coxley where, I am pleased to say, I was quite happy and I was treated as one of the family.

Three lads worked there as well as the farmer. The herd of cows was milked twice a day by hand. I also kept clean all the dairy equipment, fed the calves and the poultry. The farm grew mangolds and potatoes so we all pulled mangolds when they were fit for hauling and picked up potatoes. Then there was the haymaking. I sometimes used to think it would never end! We had double summer-time then, so we made hay for as long as we were able, after which we did the evening milking and then back to the farm to wash milking pails and udder buckets. It was about 11 o'clock or gone by then, so by the time we had supper we were glad to fall into bed. Only to be up again at 6 am!

Then came the harvesting. Every farm was expected to grow a certain amount of corn. This I quite enjoyed. There was only one tractor on the farm in those days and the rest of the work was done with horses, which I enjoyed working with.

Thelma Harding on the farm.

We milked out of doors all the year round, come rain, snow or shine. I have put my Wellington-booted foot under the cow when she had a wee more than once to warm it up! Hay was cut from ricks with a hay knife to feed the cows after milking. My knees would buckle sometimes if the 'flap' of hay was a bit heavy on my head.

It was all an experience and in February 1946 I left the Land Army and returned to my job as a typist in London, which had been kept open for me. Two years later I returned to Coxley – yes, I married a farmer's son!

My home became a poultry-breeding station
Mary Russell, Milborne Port

During the war my family lived in a small village on the Somerset/Dorset border. My father, who was a schoolteacher, had always been extremely interested in everything to do with poultry (showing, breeding, etc) and our family had always kept fowls.

I left school early to look after my family since my mother was ill. During wartime, our 'farm' became an accredited poultry-breeding station, under the Ministry of Agriculture. We kept four breeds, namely Light Sussex, Rhode Island Red, White Leghorn and Brown Leghorn. Fowls were sorted into breeding groups, each group containing twelve hens and one cockerel. Overall, we had a group of about 250 fowls.

Every time a hen went to lay in the nest box a little trap door came down and the hen had to be let out, the door reset and each egg recorded on a sheet from the numbered ring on her leg. This was a very time consuming exercise and the 'poor' layers were not bred from. We needed to have good laying strains. Once a year the Ministry vet visited to blood test every fowl on the farm. Had there been a reactor the entire flock would have been retested every four weeks until clear. Nothing was sold from the establishment until the all clear was given. There were many regulations.

We had a very large electric incubator and sent day-old chicks all over the country. They were taken early in the morning to

Milborne Port station (we had one then). They reached their destination the same day. Because we were accredited, the Ministry allowed us a larger allocation of poultry food. To supplement this we boiled up potatoes among other things in a furnace outside. We also had something called Bristol pudding delivered weekly from cooked household waste (which we mixed with the mash).

After the war, my father and I decided that we no longer wanted the red tape and paper work, so we switched to free-range poultry for egg production and produced game-cross table poultry.

I should have mentioned that on our four acres, we also kept Pansy and Chirpy, two Jersey cows.

My father was asked during the war to go around local villages and help the Dig for Victory campaign by founding horticultural societies to encourage food production. Some are still flourishing today. I used to go with him and enjoyed this immensely. In my spare time, I was a member of the Red Cross and did many hospital duties. I also belonged to the Young Conservatives and a dramatic society and altogether had a very interesting time. Two nights a week I helped at a church army canteen providing 'chat' and light refreshments to the many troops billeted in our area. I was young and it was a very exciting time.

Winter was the worst time
Mary Brill, Stoke Sub Hamdon

I attended Lincoln Girls' High School but I had to leave in 1940 to look after six horses and two ponies, which we had at that time; later two of the younger horses were taken to Aldershot where my father looked after them. Food for riding horses was becoming very difficult to buy. We humans were each issued with a ration book, which ensured a fair share of the limited supplies of food and clothing for everyone. We were very lucky living in the country, being able to keep a few chickens and two pigs. We had a large vegetable garden and an orchard, which yielded plums, apples, pears and walnuts.

We were allowed to fatten and slaughter two pigs per year. When the pig was killed it would be scraped to remove the bristles and then hung overnight in the bacon chamber, which was a large cool room above the cellar in the farmhouse. Very early next morning the butcher would arrive and cut and joint the carcass. There would be two hams, two sides and two shoulders; these would be put into a flat salting tub for curing and use during the following year. Friends would come along to help mother make sausages, haslet and brawn and to raise pork pies. My job was to clean all the intestines for use as skins for the sausages. These were made in a big mincer with a special tube attachment for threading the skins over the sausage meat as it came out of the mincer. The best leaf fat was rendered down in a large pot to make lard and the remains were made into scratchings. Very tasty! The liver, kidneys and odd pieces of meat were plated and given to helpers and neighbours, who returned the compliment when they killed their pigs; these were called fries. After two days of very hard work we were rewarded with the most delicious home-made food and a replenished larder for many months to come.

In 1943 I started work on a local farm. My first task was potato picking, oh my poor back ached so much. Then the farmer realised that I could work and manage horses. I was given the much sought after job of leading the horse and cart and driving it full of potatoes to the farmyard. When I became 18 years old I joined the Land Army but I was still doing the same kind of work. We were given some very dirty jobs, spending long hours in the fields with lots of overtime during harvest. Winter was the worst time with long bitterly cold days singling out sugar beet. Later in the year when the frosty weather started we lifted the beet out of the ground, then chopped off the tops before loading it into the carts – our gloves and hands were frozen.

From grocery shop to bakery
Betty Mitchell, Puriton

During the Second World War I was exempt from military service

as I was doing a man's job. Men always held the position of boss and second man in most grocery and provisions stores, so when they were called up we girls were given the jobs. I wanted to volunteer for military service, but my father wouldn't allow it.

The local ARP wanted volunteers so I joined them as a telephonist, doing evening shifts. We were badly bombed during the blitz on Clydeside, but thankfully things had quietened down by the time I joined. It was a case of manning the phones and being prepared for anything.

My in-laws were the village bakers here in Puriton and when I got married they asked me if I would give up my job in Scotland to help them out should their fourth son be called up, to which I agreed. Two months later the inevitable happened and I came to Puriton to work in the bakery and push hand trucks round the village delivering bread, in all kinds of weather, including snow.

Because I had changed my job the ministry tried to call me up, but father-in-law objected, and then as time went on I became pregnant so that put paid to my call-up.

Farming was in my genes
Phyllis Wyatt, Coxley & District

I volunteered for the Women's Land Army in the spring of 1941. Until then I had been working as a shorthand/typist in an office connected with the production of food (pig products – bacon, offal and NAAFI sausages) and as such was classed for employment purposes as in a reserved occupation. However, farming was in my genes and much against all the advice from my family, I found myself, early on a very frosty spring morning, cycling to work to my first posting on a farm.

I have no idea as to what some farmers and their wives considered suitable work for their land girl or if they really needed her there at all. At the first three farms to which I was sent (which covered a period of more than two years) I was, in turn, a lap dog to the wife, a confidante and go-between, and a gardener, to the point of growing roots myself. Apart from the milking twice a day, the 'General Farming' for which I had volunteered was non-existent.

By then thoroughly fed-up, on the fourth and last posting, I found myself on the farm I had been looking for.

They had a dairy of well over 30 cows. I hand-milked eight or nine cows morning and evening – in the company of the farm worker, the farmer and often with the help of one or the other of his children during school holidays.

I spread manure on the mowing pastures, cut thistles and docks with a scythe, and spent hours in the plough ground hoeing around the rot crops. I worked through the hours of double summer-time in the hayfield and was taught how to load the old 'Somerset' wooden horse-drawn wagon with pitches of hay.

I helped with the corn harvest, stooking the sheaves of wheat or oats. There were about 90 sheep on the farm; I was taught to recognise a ewe with foot rot or worms, and was given the task of counting them all and reporting back should any require attention, enjoying the responsibility this involved. I cut farm hedges with a slash hook, picked up stones before the mowing grass grew high (stones could cause damage to the mowing machine blades), picked up apples and helped with the cider making, helped when the threshing machine came – a very dirty and dusty job! – and cut withies for pea and bean sticks.

In the wintertime I had my own little dairy of eight or nine cows which were drying off but still had to be milked for a while. This was situated well away from the farm, where I fed, milked and let them out each morning from the cow house. They would have to be got in during the afternoon, tied up, fed, watered and bedded. Milking them took no time at all. They were all old friends and no trouble.

I was asked by the WLA Welfare Supervisor if I would care to take a Proficiency Test organised by Cannington Farm Institute near Bridgwater. Four of us girls on neighbouring farms said we would like to 'give it a go' and she very kindly took us there in her car. We were asked many questions relating to farming and given tasks to assess our practical capabilities. Two of us passed and were awarded a Proficiency Badge. This I still have and treasure. It was hoped our employer would also recognise our prowess and give us a half a crown rise in pay. This I duly received.

During the war years farming was still carried out in the old fashioned style which had persisted for centuries. Not many farms could boast a tractor. Horses still provided the power. It was all hard work.

I was demobbed in September 1945 but still look back at my WLA days as some of the happiest days of my life.

My ignorance with livestock was abysmal
Betty Wheller, Fivehead & District

My twin sister and I were 19 years old when war broke out in September 1939. We worked for our father who had a china, glass and hardware business in Bath and we had never been away from home.

For some time after the declaration of war, rationing had no effect and life went on much the same as usual except for the influx of Admiralty staff who had moved to Bath from London to occupy most of the lovely Georgian hotels. Their uniforms were exciting though, and so were the air force and military personnel who flooded into the city from their postings in Colerne, Box and Yatesbury etc. It was all good fun ... until one morning we received a letter marked OHMS. We had been conscripted! We were required to leave Dad's employment and do work of National Importance! We appealed against this and were granted six months' exemption. When this time elapsed we appealed again, but this time only one of us was excused. We tossed to see who should go and I lost the toss!

I opted for the Women's Land Army as being the least of the evils and I was soon packed off to the wilds of Somerset to a small dairy farm. The fact that I quickly mastered a tractor stood me in good stead, but the fact that I couldn't understand the language was a dreadful handicap. The farm hands were mostly old men who spoke in broad Somerset.

'Thee dussent' meant 'you don't', 'thee cassent' meant 'you can't' and 'thee bissent' meant 'you aren't'. When I had difficulty ploughing a straight furrow, I was told to 'Cut theeself a verk'. It eventually dawned on me that this meant, 'cut a forked stick' to use as a marker! 'Suent' meant lovely and smooth, 'turrible dobby' meant rough and uneven, 'dumpsy' meant getting dark and 'back-sunded' meant south-facing!

However, my proficiency with a tractor soon made up for my stupidity with the language and when I managed to start a neighbouring farmer's car, my stock went sky-high. At that time cars were very simple, there were no self-starters, no indicators and no ignition-start. It was required by law to immobilise them by removing the rotor-arm whenever they were parked. None of the locals had noticed the rotor-arm was missing and they had been cranking it for ages with no effect and increasing bad language! When they all walked away in disgust I quietly retrieved the rotor-arm and slipped it into place.

'Try it now lads,' I said, and of course it started at once.

'What thy land girl doanno about cars is no odds to nobody,' said the old farmer and I walked away, basking in my undeserved praise.

My ignorance with livestock was abysmal. I knew a cow gave milk but I had no idea that it had to have a calf each year before it would do so. Hand milking was extremely tiring to the hands, wrists and arms and a wop! round the ear from a manure-laden cow's tail was not the best beauty treatment in the wee small hours! The bonus, however, was an abundance of cool creamy milk.

The year unfolded and root crops came next. These had to be sown by a horse-drawn drill, which meant leading a heavy horse up and down interminable lines. As soon as the tiny leaves appeared they had to be hoed by hand and this again was a backbreaking task. Next came haymaking and this often entailed turning whole fields of mown grass manually for, of course, there were no balers then. Often the church clock struck midnight as we hauled in the last load of loose hay. The same applied to harvest. There were no combines, and wheat, barley and oats were cut with a binder and the sheaves stooked for drying and then carried to a rick or Dutch barn to await thrashing. It was all jolly hard work. I should say though that I married my boss's son and when he was demobbed we bought a small farm and continued working for the next 40 years. I didn't know when I tossed the coin that it would change the whole course of my life.

Lending a hand on the land
Eileen (Penny) White, Templecombe

I wasn't a land girl or a clippie (bus conductor). I wasn't nursing or serving in the ATS, WAAF or WRNS. I wasn't even making munitions. So what do I have to tell?

That's easy. I was rising twelve when the war began and I was one of the few children who were not evacuated, but remained in Central London for the duration. That in itself was quite an experience.

However, we were bombarded with posters, instructing us what to do to help the war effort. One of these urged us to 'Lend a Hand on the Land', and in the summer of 1943 a group of girls from my school in South London volunteered to do just that. We were all 15, not far short of 16 and longing to escape from war-torn London for a month.

Prior to this I had never been farther from London than the Kent and Sussex coast, so the West Country was new to me and very beautiful. We arrived in the late afternoon having been conveyed from the station in a lorry. We had no idea where we were, all signposts having been removed, to make life difficult for spies and fifth columnists. Eventually we disembarked, leaping off the back of the lorry and viewing the breathtaking countryside. (Oh! to be able to leap anywhere now on my worn out old knees!)

We had arrived at an empty and very dilapidated farmhouse. The first task, after we had been shown our rooms, was to collect palliasses, made out of rough sacking, go round to the back of the house where we found a straw rick, and fill the palliasses with straw. These were our beds. No one demonstrated the art of filling these properly, so that most of us spent a very uncomfortable first night, which we swiftly remedied the next day. There was nothing in the rooms at all. We slept on the bare boards and of course, we had no curtains. There was just enough space for five of us in our room. So you see the accommodation was basic to say the very least. It didn't bother us at all. Sixty years ago, our expectations were low. What did bother us was the total absence of toilet and washing facilities. I leave it to the reader's imagination how we coped.

On the morning of our first complete day, we were despatched by lorries to various farms. Here we were to help with haymaking, stooking and heaving stooks up on to the ricks, whilst the men built them. Subsequently we did some flax pulling too. Luckily it was a good summer and we enjoyed the fresh air, exercise and freedom from the war.

What interested me most was the livestock, and I watched the cows being milked (by hand, of course) and longed to get under a cow myself. Seeing my interest the farmer allowed me to wash the cows' udders prior to milking. When I eventually got to try milking I was so slow that I was soon back in the fields. Joseph, the Italian POW, was a fantastic milker; he could strip a cow in no time.

However, I digress. I've no idea how many acres this farm covered, but it was worked by the farmer, his wife, his mother-in-law, two brothers-in-law, one land girl and Joseph. I think the in-laws were there just for harvest and haymaking time.

The farmer was not young. Indeed to us he seemed ancient, but in retrospect he was probably about 60. His wife was much younger and it was obvious to us, young and innocent as we were, that she was heavily involved with Joseph, and we could understand why! In those days it was a real eye-opener to we two innocent teenagers – and, of course, we really were innocent then!

The food served at our billet was prepared and cooked (?) by domestic science students, not much older than we were. It was appalling but it's only fair to add that they had a monstrous kitchen range to cook on, which was very, very old and the results were not entirely their fault. So we were grateful to get a good midday meal on the farm, where we all sat down together *en famille*, including Joseph of course.

We worked long days before being transported back to our billet in the evenings, where we had a hurried tea and went out exploring the countryside. Most of us had borrowed bikes from the various farms and we were able to travel about along roads and lanes almost free from traffic. It was idyllic.

During our stay a large contingent of 'red berets' arrived on manoeuvres and a couple of our more mature girls were soon flirting with them. To the less adventurous of us it was quite intimidating and when they exited from the window in our room with two of the soldiers after dark, we were terrified. But there were no subsequent problems and the teachers in charge knew nothing about it. To this day my old school friend and I talk of that night and how those girls were lucky not to be raped.

Life on the farms was so quiet and peaceful that we were sad to return to London. Fortunately, we still had homes to go to, as August 1943 was not a particularly bad month for air raids.

I would not have missed that experience – it was for us town dwellers a taste of a different world and it contributed to my desire to leave London and change my life entirely, by coming to live in Somerset in 1976.

In the summer of 1944 I had a very different temporary job whilst awaiting my exam results. I spent six weeks in a factory making radar parts. The days were spent intermittently diving for shelter as this was the summer of the 'doodle bugs'. The work was excruciatingly boring and I longed for a chance to 'Lend a Hand on the Land' again.

Frosty mornings and turnips
Irene Veryard, Hadspen & Shepton Montague

I was in the Women's Land Army during the war, and have many memories of this, particularly of very early starts as having a very large dairy herd meant a 5.30 am start, as it was all hand milking. After that it was breakfast, then general farm work. My memories take me back to very frosty mornings, pulling turnips with hands so numb it almost brought tears to your eyes.

During the summer haymaking and harvest meant very long days, up to 16 hours. My pleasure was working with those shire horses, which I adore to this day.

Strawberries versus potatoes
Pam Lea, The Charltons

I went to Kings High School for Girls in Warwick. I went strawberry picking and pea picking with other girls from my school, which was fun, but potato picking was another matter. We had to follow the tractor in thick, sticky mud as it unearthed the potatoes for us to sack. It was a cold, backbreaking job and one that I never repeated!

We also helped at the local hospital, which was most satisfying as the patients really appreciated our help.

Maidie Ford was in the Timber Corp
Patricia Baynham, Watchet

Maidie, born Gladys Irene Ford in 1917, daughter of a timberman, joined the Women's Land Army in 1940 in Gilston in Wales. Most of the accommodation provided for the girls was in private digs or hostels or farms.

From Wales about 120 land girls were sent to Tirona Nurseries, cutting trees and making charcoal. The digs were primitive, but they stuck it uncomplaining for the sake of the war effort. Later, four London girls and Maidie left the nursery for Glamorgan War Agricultural Committee, being the first Land Army girls there, and were then sent onto different farms. Peggy and Blanche are still friends today.

Maidie was transferred to the Suffolk Timbercorp branch of the Land Army, then one month later sent to Northumberland to work on the Cheviot Hills in a sawmill. Later she was transferred to Dulverton Sawmills and stayed there until the end of the war.

CHAPTER 9

Manufacturing and Commerce

If Britain was to provide its fighting men with the munitions, ships, planes and equipment they needed to defeat Hitler, women had to step into those men's shoes in the manufacturing and heavy industry jobs they had been forced to leave behind. Some were volunteers, but many young women chose factory work as their 'war service' when, after December 1941, they were called up, in preference to the forces or the Women's Land Army. The work was physically exhausting, dirty, monotonous and, in some cases, positively dangerous. It was also distinctly unfeminine. No wonder finding an ex-hairdresser amongst your new colleagues was a godsend!

Mastering a capstan lathe
Betty Knight, Wiveliscombe

My mother, Gretta George, lived an idyllic life helping in her father's shop and market garden in a village in Cornwall. Then everything changed because for her war work she was directed to Hoffmans ball-bearing factory in Stonehouse, Gloucestershire, which was making bullets for the war effort.

She found the work monotonous and on the night shift it was easy to fall asleep. If the supervisor saw someone nodding off to

Gretta with her workmates.

sleep, an empty tin was dropped on the floor behind them to shock them back to alertness!

My father wrote to say his leave would be on a certain date. In the shop she only had to say to her own father, 'Jack's got leave so I'm going to visit him' and off she would go. When she said this to her supervisor she was told she would have to complete a leave request form. She did this, but didn't wait for it to be returned, she just went off and caught the train to Norfolk. When she returned she saw 'AWOL' by her name and thought it meant 'absent with official leave'!

Despite this shaky start she was soon promoted to machine setter. Now the boot was on the other foot as she found it irksome when girls who wanted a break from the boredom would deliberately bang their capstan lathe hard to put it out of alignment. They could have a break while my mother re-set it.

However, the thing which annoyed my mother most was the fact the women had to wear the same all-in-one overalls as the men. These garments had fly-fronts, which were fine for the men, but every time the women wanted to go to the toilet they had to take the whole thing off! My mother was glad when the war was over and she could return to her father's shop and wear skirts or dresses.

She never lost her mechanical skills and often helped my father and brothers repair their cars and motorbikes.

From the laundry to the National Fire Service
June Clarke, Lympsham

My life was very ordinary until September 1939. I left school at 14 in August 1938 and went to work for a builder in his office, full time, for the princely sum of 7s 6d per week. I also went to evening classes on Tuesday and Thursday evenings to learn typewriting, shorthand and accounting. At fifteen and a half in 1940 I moved to work in the office of a laundry and dry cleaners. The war had started and it was very busy, with laundry coming in from the Army and Royal Air Force. Later on also from the Americans, as we had a very big air force base nearby with bombers stationed which were bombing the Continent.

No one can imagine the great mounds of shirts, pants and socks that arrived. I was most surprised how all the items were returned to the right person; this was due to each item being marked correctly. I was in charge of the number of tickets from each man on a list, and I sent the account to the various Army and Air Force stations for payment. You can imagine the mountains of clothes in a mucky state.

I was sent for by those who wanted us women for war service three times. But each time I went for interview, my boss wrote a letter saying I was most needed where I was, so I never went into war service.

I was by this time thinking I ought to be involved with war work in some way. So I joined the Auxiliary Fire Service, later called the National Fire Service (NFS). We had a uniform, name tags and gas masks. I was 16 years old in 1940 and at that time the war was not going well. Anyway, we went for training weekends, and it was the first time I had been away from home. We were stationed, when on duty, in the Fire Station at the local Town Hall. I remember being on duty during a bad air raid. It was a very busy night with incendiaries falling everywhere. We were doing what we had been trained for, sending the fire pumps to where they were needed. We had boy messengers, aged from 15 years, on bicycles and they were also very busy riding through bad places to bring us orders from those fighting fires. The nice part was when the air raid was over; we had time to slow down. The Station Officer in charge came in and congratulated us on our way of keeping the fire service going, to keep our town safe. He said, 'Make a cup of tea for everyone', which was done and then to cap it all he brought out a bottle of whisky (well, he was the owner of the local town brewery, so he was able to get the whisky real easy). I can tell you that was the best cup of tea I have tasted in my whole life. I went on to stay in the NFS until the end of the war.

I was also concerned with sounding the air raid warnings for the whole town. The factory where I worked had a siren, which could be used for this. There were two girls on duty in the laundry office all night, in turn. We would get a phone call saying 'Air Raid Warning Yellow', when it was preparing us for what was to come, then 'Air Raid Warning Red' and then one of us, which had to be me at this time, had to go through the factory to pull the cord at the required times. There was a special order of counts, and everybody could hear this siren in the whole town and go to shelter. When we got

the signal 'Air Raid Warning Green', we had to return to pull the cord so that everybody knew the air raid was over.

All this had to be done in the dark, which was very frightening. As you got more experienced it got a little easier.

Another experience was having a lot to do with the Americans when they were stationed near us. They used to make us very envious, as they didn't have rationing like us. They used to throw candy at us office girls, which we thanked them for. We were very short of everything through rationing, so when we were invited to their dances, we saw doughnuts and oranges, things we hadn't seen for a very long time. The Americans were very polite to us and we got on very well.

I am sure that I grew up a lot quicker owing to the war and I am a lot better for it.

My mother made camouflage nets
Doris Neville, Ash

Although only a child during the war, I remember my mother, Elsie Bennett, was employed at 'Kelways' in Langport, making camouflage nets for the forces. She had to cycle four miles each way, every day to do this work. The nets had to be made exactly to pattern as the forces' lives depended on them when in use. She also packed egg powder. I have heard her say the first thing they did when they got to work was to bang the heaps of nets and skrim (that is the material the nets were made from) to get rid of the rats which had got in over night. She then became a postwoman towards the end of the war.

Starting out as an office junior at Charles Dye & Co
Betty Bowles, East Chinnock

I started work in 1942 when I was 14 years old at a motor cycle components works called Charles Dye & Co in Sherborne Road,

Yeovil. At this time I was living in Fordhay Terrace, East Chinnock. Every day I caught the Safeway bus at 8 am to start work at 9 am; the fare was 8d return. I finished work at 6 pm and caught the 6.10 pm bus home. I worked Saturday mornings till 1 pm.

I started work as the junior; my duties were filing, folding the invoices and putting them in envelopes, stamping them and taking to the Post Office in Middle Street. One of my duties in the morning was to go to the nearest cake shop in Middle Street and buy cakes for the office staff; I used to borrow my workmate's bike to do this, with my gas mask over my shoulder. When I arrived back to the office I used to make the tea for about ten people in the office. After about one year, another girl started work as the junior and I learnt to type the invoices, working out the percentage discount and adding all the figures etc.

East Chinnock did not suffer any damage during the war. When my father heard the sirens he told us to go to the understairs cupboard. I remember the bombing at Houndstone Camp; the flames could be seen from East Chinnock and that time we sheltered in a neighbour's underground air raid shelter. When the centre of Yeovil was bombed I remember going to work the next day and seeing the destruction; several people were killed.

Socials were held in the village school. The band consisted of local talent, men from West Coker joined the East Chinnock men to provide music for the evening and they played at other villages as well.

We had to be very exact in our work
Dorothy Sydenham, Bickenhall & District

For my work I was directed to work away from home. I was in engineering at Brake & Signals in Chippenham. The work was dirty and cold and the shop steward brought us out on strike once because of the conditions.

The machine I was on was a Horizontal Miller. We had to be very exact in our work, everything was inspected. We were making parts for guns, planes and ships. I was in a team with men. We worked two weeks on day shift, 7.30 am to 7 pm, with an hour for lunch. Then we went onto night shift 7.30 pm to 7 am, with two half-hour breaks.

To work we stood on duckboards on a concrete floor, wearing overalls as some protection against oil splashing and swarf spitting from the machine. Each job done was priced so 'Don't work too fast', the men would say, but the bosses wanted work done 'ASAP'. The firms they were making parts for had 'chasers' around, speeding them up; Rolls Royce was one such firm.

Phyl Scott made Spitfire tails
Liz Henley, West Buckland

Phyl Scott was married at the age of 23 and was 25 years old in 1939 when the war started. She lived at 26, William Street, Taunton, by the station.

Phyl volunteered to work at Avimo at the beginning of the war. It was a family affair; her husband, father and brother also worked at Avimo helping to make Spitfires. In addition Phyl had to have a lady war worker billeted with her who was also employed at Avimo. Phyl was employed making Spitfire tails. The frames for the tails were constructed rather like Meccano. All the workers were on piecework and Phyl's work partner suggested that if she held the rivets in the holes and he hammered them in they would construct the tails a lot quicker and earn more money. The only drawback being that Phyl suffered sore fingers and thumbs when he missed!

Unfortunately, Phyl then hurt her back and had to give up this work. Phyl then had evacuees from London billeted with her; Joan Platt and Joyce Smith were just nine years old. Eventually Joan went back to London but Joyce stayed two to three years. One night her mother, two sisters and an aged aunt turned up on Phyl's doorstep from London looking for shelter as a 'doodle bug' had landed and lodged under their doorway. Phyl put them up for

Helping to make Spitfires was all part of a woman's work.

the night while accommodation was found for them as they had nowhere to live.

In addition to this, in 1942 Phyl and her husband Les were fireguards for William Street which was near Taunton Railway Station and Potters Builders Yard, which was full of wood and would be a fire hazard, Les being party leader and Phyl his deputy. The fire-fighting parties were organised by Taunton Town Council and Phyl still has the certificate authorising her husband to carry out these duties.

The evacuees went back and then the Americans arrived in Taunton at Norton Manor Camp. It was a Good Friday morning when Phyl learnt that she was to have an American soldier billeted with her called Eugene Hendricks, who stayed three months and then went back to Hotsprings, Arkansas, USA.

Although these were worrying times, life did have its lighter moments. Like many people, Phyl had an air raid shelter in her garden. One night when the sirens went, Les got up quickly and dressed, only to find out sometime later that he had his trousers on back to front!

Morale boosting at the Woolwich Arsenal
Veronica Andrews, Stoke St Gregory

My mother Hazel Farmer could not believe her eyes. What a difference a day made. Yesterday she was the youngest manager of a hairdressing salon in the West End of London; today she was starting work at the Woolwich Arsenal. At the end of 1943 all hands were needed to fuel the tanks, aeroplanes and ships that were striving to bring victory in the war, so everyone was called upon to do duty for the war effort. Hazel had been expecting the call for some time and had been surprised that it had taken so long. She did realise, though, that keeping spirits high on the home front was also looked upon as 'war effort', especially when you were 'called up' to work as a freelance hairdresser with Gainsborough Pictures!

This was something completely different. For a start the noise and dirt were something to behold! The group of women she was to work with had all been there since the war began and were hardened to the working atmosphere – the language was ripe and the humour caustic! They looked with disbelief on this smart young woman who looked as though she's never done a day's work in her life and wondered how the heck she'd survive, but Hazel was not daunted, she buckled down and showed that she could work with the best of them.

One lunchtime they got to talking about their lives before the war and were amazed to hear that Hazel had been a hairdresser. A thought came to a few of them and they cornered the manager and somehow, don't ask how, got him to agree that a small room should be set aside and equipped (by fair means or foul) with everything needed to bring a hairdressing salon to the factory. When everything was in place, Hazel began to provide the morale boost the girls craved for. After all, who wouldn't want to look their best when the Yanks were in town! The girls would go out to the pictures, see a style they liked and Hazel would provide it when the next date had been arranged. In the end the few men working in the factory also came along as well – they didn't want to be left out.

Unfortunately it all ended when Hazel got married in June 1944 and had to leave the factory for pastures new. She was given a rousing send off and a lovely present of a Waterford crystal cake stand (goodness only knows where the girls got that from!), but I have it still – a constant reminder of the good times my mother had with her friends in the munitions factory.

From blood donor to factory worker
Winifred Morse, Kilmersdon

During the war I first worked at the Doctor's house and did all sorts of jobs. He asked me if I would give blood at the Victoria Hall in Radstock – when I got back he gave me a bar of Cadbury's milk chocolate!

My next job was at Prattens where I donned overalls and gloves and was put to work on a large crosscut saw, cutting timber for prefab housing. My friend was on a six-hole driller, as both men whose jobs these were had joined the army. We also made ammunition boxes.

During the evening I belonged to the WVS and ARP, going round checking blackouts. We used to cook meals in dustbins supported on bricks – we once made stew and apple pie for evacuees, which we served in an old garage. We learnt first aid and had gas mask drill. We had to go everywhere on our bikes, even to dances. We would tuck our long skirts under a belt and off we went.

CHAPTER 10

Top Secret

Sometimes war work was so secret that even now, 60 years on, the women involved find it impossible to talk about. An 18 year old school leaver might find herself at 'Station X', the now famous code-breaking centre at Bletchley Park, or working for MI6 or the American War Office. Our own War Office at Whitehall relied on female staffing, and girls with a head for figure work were snapped up by the Inland Revenue or the many companies struggling to provide utilities and services on the Home Front.

I worked at Station X

Moyna Snelson, Ilminster

I still cannot really tell you what I did for two years during the Second World War because it was secret work. At 18, having taken my Higher School Certificate, I set off in September 1943 to work in the British Cryptanalytical headquarters at Bletchley Park, or Station X as it was known. This was a Victorian mansion in Buckinghamshire – the Allies' top-secret centre for deciphering enemy codes; where brilliant men and women broke the ingenious Enigma cipher; where Alan Turing was the brains behind the world's first programmable computer and ordinary people like me did our shift's work and never said a word about what we did.

Station X.

We lived in billets in outlying villages, mine was Newport Pagnell. We attended musical recitals and drama performances, social evenings and dances in a hall attached to Bletchley House. We grew up, fell in love and missed out on our teenage years, but in later times we learnt that Churchill described us as his 'secret weapon' that shortened the war – and I knew it was all worth while.

───◦◈◦───

From secretarial school to MI6
Janet Baillie, The Charltons

I was 18 when war broke out and I had just left school having taken my Higher School Certificate examinations.

It was then decided that I should get some secretarial training and I went to Mrs Hoster's College in London and did shorthand, typing, some bookkeeping and French! So I travelled up to Victoria station every day on the Southern Railway from Cheam. Then I got a job in an accountant's office with four partners and being the only employee I was given the office key to open it up each day. By this time the bombing raids on London were getting worse. Everywhere was blacked out; so were the station names and there was no announcement by railway staff as to where you were on your journey. I did not bother to count the stations we stopped at until after Hackbridge because that was where the anti-aircraft guns were always firing.

I had been working in the accountant's office in Walbrook near St Paul's Cathedral for some time when I got a letter from Mrs. Hoster's College asking me to attend an interview in a Government office. I went and to my surprise (I can now tell you) it turned out to be MI6 under another name. Do not get any big ideas – I was only a typist!

I left the accountant's office in the City on the Friday and on the Saturday there was the raid which resulted in that well known photograph of St Paul's remaining intact and everything burning all round. On the Monday I started my new job near St James' Park and I found I still had the old office key! I got permission to take the key back to the accountant's during the lunch hour the next day. I got a bus but I could not get anywhere near Walbrook. The whole street with the accountant's office had been destroyed. I shall never forget the lines of spaghetti, so many hoses, on a bridge. I have still got the office key!

My most frightening experience was when I was travelling on the Underground to get back to Victoria station and I was squashed in the train with so many people I could not get out at the next station. Indeed no one could get out because there were so many people on the platform. The train went past two stations before we could get out and then I had to get back to Victoria station, which fortunately was still there and the trains to Cheam were still running. It was not only frightening for me; it was frightening for my parents because there were no mobile phones then.

The American War Office and a buzz bomb
Mona Coupland, South Molton

My friend Gretta and I did everything together so I was lost when Gretta was called up to go to Stonehouse in Gloucestershire, to work in a factory, munitions I think. I was in a reserved occupation, in an accountant's office and was twice held back, but was finally conscripted to work in the American War Office in Cheltenham. I was given a shorthand test, but never asked to use it!

Now that Gretta and I were both in Gloucestershire, I had a day off and decided to visit her. It was quite a journey, changing buses at Gloucester and Stroud, and I planned to surprise her. However, I had the surprise – when I eventually found the building where Gretta was a supervisor I was told she had gone to Cheltenham to visit me! I hurried back to the hostel to find Gretta was still there so we did meet up for a while.

I later moved to London with the American War Office and worked in Grosvenor Square, often walking to the Square from the Green Cross Residential Club at Primrose Hill, through Regents Park and Baker Street. The windows of the club were all boarded up when we first arrived due to all the glass being broken by explosions. Great rejoicing one day, all the glass had been replaced. The very next day it was all broken by a nearby buzz-bomb. An open-air church service was held every week and on one occasion, General Eisenhower attended.

A friend, Dorothy, and I had a near miss with a buzz-bomb when walking by the Thames. It fell in the water close to us and we were thrown to the ground with the force, shaken but unhurt.

The war changed my life – I never expected to leave Cornwall, but married a soldier from Lincolnshire and lived there for ten years before moving to Devon.

My time at the War Office
Christine Ellen, Westbury-sub-Mendip

When the war began, I was a teenager at school in Woking,

Surrey. I had just obtained my School Certificate (the equivalent of GCSE) and was hoping to train as a librarian. I stayed on for a year, during which we shared our premises with a school from Putney, each group using the school for three days a week, taking lessons in various private houses on the days when we could not occupy the buildings.

It became obvious during 1940 that, with compulsory war work for women, my chosen career was not going to be possible, and in the autumn of that year I started a six-month's secretarial course at St Godric's Secretarial College, evacuated from Hampstead to Watford in Hertfordshire. In the spring of 1941 I obtained a post as a Grade 1 shorthand typist at the War Office in Whitehall, where I started in the main typing pool in early summer. I had been fortunate in finding a boarding house in Hampstead, from which I could travel daily into work by bus or tube.

The girls and women in the typing pool were a mixed bag; some were permanent Civil Servants but most of us were wartime employees. Some girls worked for specific branches, a large group of us was on call for anyone who asked, some were copy-typists only and there was a group who sat at the back of the room typing stencils for the Gestetner machines down in the basement. When I had been working for a fortnight, I received an official letter saying that, as I was still under 18, I could not be paid as a Grade 1 shorthand writer, with the result that I could only receive 30 shillings a week plus overtime. As I had to pay 22 shillings a week rent and had travel expenses, this made life difficult, but there it was: Grade 1 I might be, but to the Civil Service I was Grade 2 until I was 18!

Much of the work was routine letters, beginning 'Dear Sir, I am directed to state ...' and ending 'I am, Sir, your most obedient servant ...'. The shorthand work was more interesting, involving contact with some interesting characters. One Major, for whom nobody wanted to work, used to throw one a file and say, 'Write and tell him he can't have it!' I liked him but many of the girls were frightened of him, as it involved reading the correspondence in the file and replying in the usual stock phrases used, which were soon learnt. I once had to take a long dictation on a report on a captured German tank, full of technical details, and went down with the 'flu the next day, which meant that someone else had to type from my shorthand. Luckily, I had not had time to acquire a lot of idiosyncrasies and my shorthand was very neat; so they were able to decipher it, with some difficulty, as they were not slow to point out when I returned.

Working hours were nine to six, with one day a week when we had to work late, going in late in the morning and working until 9 pm. Lunch could be obtained in the War Office canteen and there was any number of cafes and restaurants in the area, most of which I visited, from Lyon's Corner House in the Strand to Vega in Leicester Square; but the best was the one run by the WVS at the National Gallery where you could get an excellent meal. There was always one picture from the collection on show for a month in the foyer, and there were lunchtime concerts, given by musicians such as Myra Hess. My social life was mainly spent in the West End, where there were plenty of concerts, plays, opera and ballet and, in the summer, the Proms, which went on magnificently and which I enjoyed very much.

I spent one week in Piccadilly at the Insurance Branch and a fortnight on the Second Floor. This was where all the prestigious offices were situated and the letters were typed on the best crested notepaper. It was while I was there that I discovered I had head lice, much to my horror. I visited the little American Drug Store in Northumberland Avenue and was given a bottle of pungent lotion, which fortunately worked very quickly.

One interesting assignment was when I was sent to work for Eric Linklater, who had written *The Defence of Calais*, which we had typed out in the typing pool. He was dictating letters of thanks to various people who had helped him. When I entered the very crowded little room where he was temporarily housed, there were no chairs to spare; and he very kindly gave me his and sat upon the windowsill. I enjoyed typing his letters more than typing his book, because although his handwriting was one of the most difficult I had ever had to decipher, his manners were perfect.

We had our moments of excitement: there was the day when the lady supervising us rushed in calling, 'Girls! We've sunk the Bismarck!' And we all cheered. On another occasion there was a loud scream from one of the girls as a large rat emerged from under her desk. When I wrote to the Principal of my Secretarial College to tell her about my Grade 1/Grade 2 problem, I mentioned this episode but she was horrified, both by my treatment by the Finance branch and the working conditions, and offered to find me another job. She had advised us, however, before we left college, to stay in our first job for six months if possible, as we could claim 'experience'; so I decided to stay put, and as it happened, this was the right decision.

In November I was transferred to Horse Guards, to work for an Anti-Aircraft branch. This promotion coincided with my eighteenth birthday and an increase in pay, bringing my income to over £2 a week, at which point I had to pay income tax. We were all promised post-war credits – I finally received mine in middle age.

Horse Guards was an interesting rabbit warren, with long, narrow corridors with sharp bends, rather dark in places. Part of it was bomb-damaged and unusable, but the room where I worked looked out on Whitehall on one side and the back garden of No 10 Downing Street on the other. The branch was a Royal Artillery group concerned in mobilising units and contained a varied collection of wartime soldiers, officers and other ranks. There was a Lieutenant Colonel, a lawyer in civil life, who had a room to himself; two Majors, one of them a lawyer, the other from the publishing world; a Captain concerned with personnel welfare, a Lieutenant Quartermaster and an ATS Junior Commander, all in one room; several Army clerks, three female civilians and myself in the adjoining room, with the typist and more Army clerks in a small room beyond. We were all supervised by the Sergeant Major.

I shared a group of three desks and when I arrived there was no chair for me; the other girl, Joy, who arrived with me, had no light bulb over her table. The bombardier occupying the desk on my left, tut-tutted and went off to find these necessities and took them from the desk on my right.

'I don't know what he'll say when he comes back,' he commented. 'You've got his chair and she's got his light bulb ...'

'Oh,' we said, 'is there another one of you?'

'Oh, yes,' he replied. 'He's easier on the eyes than we are. All the girls fall for him.' He studied Joy. 'You won't,' he prophesied, and 'You will' as he looked at me.

I soon got to know my fellow workers: the Sergeant Major was a good organiser and ran the office well but was a bully with a short fuse. The female clerks were friendly; Joy became a great friend, although we had little in common, her life being full of ups and downs and always with a boyfriend. The bombardier was very entertaining – he was a wartime soldier and had worked for *Weldon's Ladies Journal*. He could not close his left eye and was no use at all with a rifle and the obvious place for him was as a clerk. He had a wicked sense of humour and his conversation was full of subtle innuendoes. The officers varied very much in their methods of work, some straightforward, but one in particular was a dreadful man to take dictation from as he kept on changing his mind. He became aware that this irritated me and used to tease me about it. The Colonel was the easiest – a man with a really untidy desk who could always find what he was looking for and never wasted time. They all had a dreadful habit of discussing anything important over tea and wanting it all done by six o'clock.

The thing I found most difficult to take was the extremely bad language and coarse jokes of some of the soldiers – I had obviously lived a very sheltered life – but it was important not to appear shocked. I learnt quite a lot at this stage. Repartee had never been my strong point but I received a good training in it in this department.

One social custom in this office was that if any of the soldiery were promoted, we all went out for a beer after work, usually at the Duncannon in Northumberland Avenue, or the Northumberland in the passage going up to Charing Cross Station. The first time this happened I drank my half-pint in terror that it would make me drunk; of course, it didn't and I got used to these occasions. Later, one dark night after one of these celebrations, I came out of the pub in the blackout and walked slap into the double-sided pillar-box, which stood right in the middle of the passage. Needless to say, I collected a lovely bruise on my face, which took some living down!

I had been in the branch about a week when the aforementioned heart-throb returned from leave, fortunately after a new chair and light bulb had been procured, so there were no recriminations. He was a Staff Sergeant, known as Douggie to the office, although his first name was Walter. The Bombardier had been correct: he was very good-looking and pleasant in his manners. Before long, we discovered mutual interests: music, opera and ballet. He had been a supporter of Sadlers' Wells Theatre before the war, belonged to the Vic-Wells Association and was able to obtain tickets to the ballet at the New Theatre. This opened up a new world for me and I spent all my spare money on ballet tickets, much to my mother's disapproval.

I used to go home at the weekend if possible and sometimes, when I had to work on Sundays, I travelled home on Sunday night from Waterloo to Woking, caught the bus to Knaphill, and walked the last half-mile home in pitch darkness. We had never had street lighting in Bisley, so this was no problem. Life was much safer for young girls on their own than it is now; I used to wander all over London on my own in the dark and no one molested me. I had the occasional request to go for a walk with a strange man, for which I had plenty of excuses, and later, when I had moved to Bayswater, I was often asked to direct Canadian soldiers to the Canadian Club in Leicester Gardens, where I lived.

Gradually I acquired a more fashionable wardrobe, under Joy's influence – there were plenty of reasonably priced attractive clothes if one chose carefully. I acquired a shepherd's plaid suit with a Gor-ray skirt, a style with elaborately cut pleats, which swung nicely and was very flattering to the figure. In common with most of the women, I used to unpick old knitted sweaters, wash the wool and re-knit in a new pattern. Fair-Isle was popular because it used up all the oddments. We all wore rayon stockings if we wore any at all which, with the shortage of clothing coupons, was often the case. I can remember going without stockings in quite cold weather. We had to mend the ladders in those days, too! Shoes were also a problem; most of us only had two pairs, one for work and one for leisure activities. Attractive underwear was difficult to find, mostly made of Celanese, fine knitted rayon, soft and comfortable but rather given to holiness.

The lucky girls were the attachments of RAF pilots, who received presents of silk stockings and later in the war, nylon ones from foreign parts.

The house at Hampstead became very crowded and I was asked to share a room with four other people, as my room was needed for someone who could pay more rent. I did not care for this at all and moved to the club in Bayswater, where I shared with one other girl for 30 shillings a week. It was a mixed club, occupying two houses, between which ran the District Line underground, disguised at street level by a false stucco facade, which looked like all the other houses in the street. The rooms were more comfortable than those at Hampstead but the house suffered from a similar shortage of bathrooms and the one near my room had a fearsome geyser which terrified me. My roommate was a Yorkshire girl, an engineering student working in the London Office of Head Wrightson. We became very good friends and we used to swap sweaters to vary our wardrobe – she was much taller than I was so we were a bit limited.

The other occupants of the club came from all parts and were working in wartime jobs all over London, but among the younger people were some medical students from St Mary's who, on one occasion, gave a New Year's Eve party to which nearly everyone went. Between them, they had managed to acquire numerous bottles of wine. I was not a great drinker and only had two drinks that evening, but what they were I don't know, apart from being two very different drinks. Suffice it to say that when I awoke the next morning the ceiling came down to meet me and I felt dreadful. I proceeded to the office as usual and on mentioning my situation to Staff Sergeant Ellen, received the reply, 'You've got a hangover – you'll be all right by mid-morning. Go and have a coffee.' This slightly unsympathetic comment was quite true and I recovered remarkably quickly; but at later parties I always stuck to the same drink!

I now travelled to work on the Circle Line from Queensway to Victoria and walked through St James' Park to work. On days when I was working late and had plenty of time I used to walk all the way, through Kensington Gardens, Hyde Park, Green Park and St James' and this was wonderful on spring and summer mornings. Once, on crossing Horse Guards' Parade, I was nearly run down by a large car turning out of the Downing Street side, and noticed that the occupant in the back was Winston Churchill!

My aunt worked for the Inland Revenue
Nancy Cox, Ilminster

My aunt, Mary House, was married on 20th January, 1940 after working for the Inland Revenue from the age of 17. She had to leave the Civil Service as at that time no married women were employed. Her husband's work was in Reading and by then Reading was full of evacuees and they had great difficulty in finding a house to rent; there were none left to buy.

Her husband volunteered for the RAF early in 1941. By then the Inland Revenue was pressing for married women to go back, so she did and worked in Reading until just before her son was born in February 1943. For part of that time she was seconded to the Regional Commissioner's Office. Because she was working and living alone, no children were billeted on her but she had a series of grown-ups. A lady who smoked and drank heavily, a French girl working at the BBC Monitoring Station nearby, a teacher-headmistress and her mother evacuated with her school from London and a lady from the local Billeting Office. There were problems with some, but others remained friends for life.

They dealt with rationing, queued for shortages and sometimes had the threat of their electricity and water being cut off. Their large garden was very hard work but a joy in keeping them with a fairly good supply of vegetables and fruit.

We all got on well together at the Gas Company
Queenie Gibbins, Martock

When I had to register in 1940 for war work I put in for the Land Army, but was refused because I had always done figure work, being Chief Cashier and Bookkeeper in a big high-class grocer's. So I was put forward to the South Suburban Gas Company, and had to go for an interview at their Head Office in Sydenham, plus a medical. I got through it all and started work at Bexley Heath Gas Company in the Broadway very near to where I lived. It was all so strange with lots of young girls and three men, all the gas collectors and engineers. They were a great bunch of workers who were very happy and we all got on well together.

Every girl in the office had her own job to do; I with three others had to check the work sheets of all the outside collectors and get the cards of each customer out of the filing cabinets and enter up all the details. Others checked the cash from the meters when collected. We also dealt with phone calls and queries. We often spent time working down in the big concrete shelter in the yard, which was quite deep. We had a chappie called Dick who was our watcher on the roof and if he sounded his huge whistle, or the siren went we all left the office and raced down four flights of stairs, out the back door, across the yard and into the shelter. We stayed in the shelter until the all clear sounded, which sometimes would be an hour or more.

We all volunteered for fire watch duty of a night, also Saturday and Sunday evenings. If the siren went we went up onto the roof to watch for any fires, hoping no bombs would rain down on us. We got one shilling for each night we did. My desk mate and I liked doing Saturday nights as the three men also did Saturdays and they were great table tennis buffs, so we got to enjoy playing, should the night be a little peaceable.

I met the President's wife
Joan Wood, Buckland St Mary

When war was declared I was living in South Croydon with my parents. I was working in an accountant's office in Budge Row opposite Cannon Street station in London and studying to become an accountant. I was approached to join a committee that had been set up by Diana Marr-Johnson, the daughter of the then

Lord Chancellor, to help families with small children, who had been in bombed areas and needed help/homes etc.

There were five committees set up to cover the country and the H.Q. was at Beecham Lodge, near Paddington. Help was needed very quickly in the London area because bombing had already started and happened nearly every night. I was appointed secretary to the London/South East committee and we started immediately.

A school was offered by a Belgian order of nuns who were taking their pupils (boarders, mostly) to Dorset. They offered us two large houses in West Byker in Surrey and use of any of the equipment they could not take with them. That together with a grant from the Lord Mayor's Air Raid Distress Fund and a large donation from West America enabled us to open as quickly as possible. Staff were the greatest problem, nurses were at a premium, but we managed to find a good organiser to get things going and there was no shortage of patients. London was being bombed nightly and the poorer areas were being hit regularly.

Children came to us up to the age of five years and we looked after them until relatives were found or if necessary, permanent arrangements were made. Towards the end of 1944 when things were quieter the convent wanted their houses back. We managed to buy a property in Sandhurst, Berkshire and used it as a convalescent home for children, with the staff we had collected. A few years after the war it was given to Berkshire County Council, who ran it for many years.

One interesting thing – I was invited to meet the Chairman of our American benefactors in London, as she was on a visit to England. She turned out to be Mrs Roosevelt! She was delightful, and pleased with our success.

INDEX

INDEX

INDEX